PRO ETO
ПРО ЭТО
That's What

Vladimir Mayakovsky

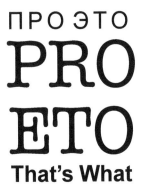

ПРО ЭТО

PRO

ETO

That's What

Alexander Rodchenko

Translated by
Larisa Gureyeva & George Hyde

Introduced by
John Wakeman

PUBLICATIONS
2009

Published by Arc Publications,
Nanholme Mill, Shaw Wood Road
Todmorden OL14 6DA, UK

The poem 'Pro Eto' by Vladimir Mayakovsky
was first published in *LEF,* 1923.
Translation copyright © Larisa Gureyeva
& George Hyde 2009

Design by Tony Ward
Printed by Lightning Source

Scan to read this book in other formats
978 1904614 31 9 (paperback)
978 1904614 71 5 (hardback)
978 1908376 38 1 (ebook)

ACKNOWLEDGMENTS
The Russian text of *Pro Eto* is reproduced from the
original version published in *LEF* in 1923.
The photomontages by Alexander Rodchenko, produced
in collaboration with the poet and first published in mono-
chrome, are here reproduced in their original colour version
by kind permission of the Director of The State Museum of
V. V. Mayakovsky, Moscow.

The cover design is an adaptation of the cover of the original
edition of 1923, Rodchenko's portrait of Lily Brik.
Reproduced by kind permission of the Director of
The State Museum of V. V. Mayakovsky, Moscow.

The publishers acknowledge financial assistance
from ACE Yorkshire

LOTTERY FUNDED

**Arc Classics: New Translations of Great Poetry of the Past
Series Editor: Philip Wilson
Translations Editor: Jean Boase-Beier**

Посвящается ей и мне.
Dedicated to her and to me.

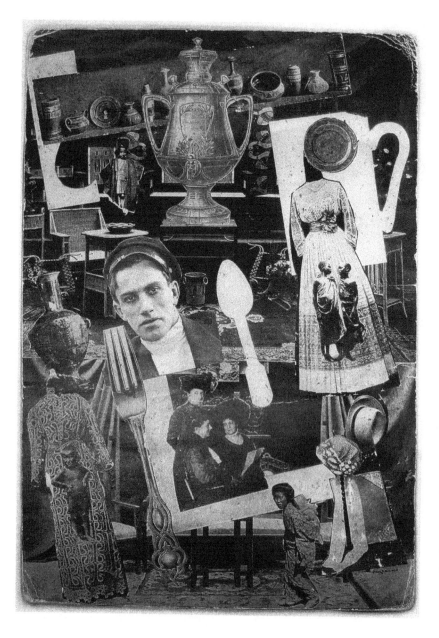

Although Alexander Rodchenko produced the above illustration [untitled] as part of his series of photomontages for *Pro Eto – That's What*, it did not appear in the first published edition.

VLADIMIR MAYAKOVSKY AND
THAT'S WHAT

The long love poem called here *That's What* is entitled in Russian *Pro Eto*, which literally means "About This", with the strong suggestion that the author felt the need to defend himself against the criticism that had come his way for the irregular nature of his unconventional love-life. Typically, the Russian words carry echoes of the words for "poet" and "proletarian" as well as expressing a characteristic off-hand defiance which is a sort of protective colouring. Love, the class struggle, technological change and the creative process itself all fuse together in what George Hyde identified, in his translation of Mayakovsky's *How Are Verses Made* (1926), [a] as the "expanded metaphors" typical of this poet's work. Indeed, Mayakovsky's elaborate incremental metaphors and metonymies reflect, in this poem as in all his work, the creative fascination with sound and form and linguistic metamorphosis and variation that made him a sort of "poet's poet", the doyen, if not the envy, of other poets (Pasternak, for example) who by no means shared his revolutionary political convictions and commitments.

Mayakovsky's empathy with the urban poor was born of experience. The son of a forest ranger, born in 1893 in Georgia, he was forced to move with his family to Moscow after his father's sudden death. The world of rented rooms and poverty, intensified subsequently in *That's What* by communist Moscow's painful attempts to catch up with modernity, is matched by the creativity of a brilliant artistic imagination engaging in its own way with the verbal and visual experiments of Futurism, Constructivism, Formalism and the host of other feverishly creative "isms" that have made Russian Modernism so powerfully influential in world art. In the winter of 1913-1914 the Futurists, with whom Mayakovsky identified, had toured Russia, reading their work to large and sometimes hostile audiences. Mayakovsky, with his huge build, huger voice and flamboyant clothes, was himself a

---

[a] V. Mayakovsky, *How Are Verses Made?* [hereafter *HVM*] (Cape, 1970).

7

"slap in the face of public taste", (the title of a Futurist manifesto) and revelled in the role, which he went on to combine with his own unique formulation of the unfallen spirit of the revolution.

His extremely personal style was developing rapidly. He hated "fine writing", prettiness and sentimentality, and went to the opposite extreme, employing the rough talk of the streets, deliberate grammatical heresies and all kinds of neologisms, which he turned (in *HVM*) into a compendium of revolutionary rhetoric aimed at aesthetic victory in the class war. He wrote much blank verse, but also made brilliant (almost untranslatable) use of a rich variety of rhyme schemes, assonance and alliteration, creating complex patterns. His rhythms are powerful but irregular, departing from the syllabo-tonic principle of Russian versification, and based on the number of stressed syllables in a line, rather like Hopkins's dynamic-archaic "sprung rhythm", and influenced by Whitman and Verhaeren. In his public readings, he would often declaim in a staccato "that's what" take-it-or-leave-it style, indicated typographically by the use of very short lines, spilling down the page in a distinctive "staircase" shape which also turns into a narrative principle, analysed by Victor Shklovsky: [b]

> Hey, you!
>> You fine fellows who
>>> Dabble in sacrilege
>>>> In crime
>>>>> In violence!

[b] Shklovsky's 'The Connection between Devices of Sjuzhet Construction and General Stylistic Devices (1919), reprinted in Bann and Bowlt, eds., *Russian Formalism* (Scottish Academic Press, 1973), acknowledges Lily's husband Osip Bric as the inspiration for the concept of the "staircase" structure as being all-important in literary language, which is characterised by repetition, parallelism, retardation, peripeteia (changes of direction with "plot" significance) etc. – much as a staircase, as one ascends or descends, turns away from and against itself while maintaining a forward momentum in several directions at once. The complex simultaneous space-time structure of stairs inspired many Modernist artists.

Have you seen
       The most terrible thing?
               My face, when
                       I
                               Hold myself calm? [c]

Strangely akin to modern rock poetry in its erotic thrust and
bluesy complaints and cries of pain, not to mention its sardonic
humour, Mayakovsky's poetry is aggressive, mocking and ten-
der all at once, and often fantastic or grotesque. His imagery is
violent and hyperbolic – he speaks of himself (for example) as
"vomited by a consumptive night into the palm of Moscow" [d]
The figure of Mayakovsky himself towers at the centre of his
poems, martyred by fools and knaves, betrayed by love, prepos-
terous or tragic, abject or heroic, but always larger than life, a
giant among midgets. Characteristically, his first book, a collection of four poems published in 1913, was called "Ya" ("I"). In
his "autobiographical tragedy" *Vladimir Mayakovsky* (1913), he
portrayed the poet romantically as a prophet in heroic conflict
with the banality of everyday life (the Russian word for this is
"byt", and it recurs in his suicide poem.) It played to packed
houses despite exorbitant ticket prices. After the revolution,
Mayakovsky's poetry, like Meyerhold's theatre, spoke directly
to huge proletarian audiences. It was Meyerhold who staged (in
1918) Mayakovsky's *Mystery-Bouffe*, a typically subversive and
blasphemous rewriting of the story of Noah reaching his prom-
ised land. The epic narratives of travel and escape that figure so
prominently in *That's What* are prefigured in the epic (or mock-
epic) poem about American interventionism entitled *150,000,000*
(1919-1920), in which the folk-hero Ivan fights a hand-to-hand

[c] Or in Reavey and Hayward's translation: "the terror of terrors – / my
face / when / I / am absolutely calm. *The Bedbug and Selected Poetry*,
(Meridian Books, 1960), p. 71.
[d] Or in Reavey and Hayward's translation: "coughed up by a consumptive night on the dirty hand of the Presnya." *op. cit.* p. 95.

battle with Woodrow Wilson, resplendent in a top hat as high as the Eiffel Tower. Folk tale and political satire fuse in the name of the proletariat (the hundred and fifty million Soviet citizens.)

His most popular poem among present-day Russian readers, however, is undoubtedly the pre-revolutionary *Oblako v Shtanakh* (The Cloud in Trousers, 1915). Its dramatic gestures of despair at being rejected by Maria, his lover, (actually a composite figure), prefigure the more complex and extended masochistic narratives of humiliation and defeat in *That's What*. In both poems the poet's suffering grows to become a paradigm of all the rejection and dispossession in the world, and his rage swells to encompass art, religion and the entire social order, until he is threatening to bring the whole world crashing down in revenge for his failure in love, and the social conspiracy which has cheated him of the object of his overwhelming (Oedipal?) desire. The intensity of these emotions carried him close to madness, and found its "objective correlative" in the creative and destructive energies of the revolution. George Hyde discusses in his Preface the intermittently happy, ultimately destructive *ménage à trois* he conducted with Osip and Lily Brik, recorded in painful detail in a recent play by Steve Trafford, *A Cloud in Trousers*[e] and echoed in many sequences of *That's What*. She did not reject him, but neither did she reciprocate his immoderate love, or give up other admirers. For sixteen years Mayakovsky publicly lamented Lily's coldness and inconstancy, beginning just a few months after their first meeting with *The Backbone Flute* (1915). But what he *really* wanted from her, at the end of the day, it would be hard to say.

All of this disproportionate, insatiable orality helps us to understand why Mayakovsky welcomed the Russian revolution as "my" revolution and why he resisted (as he does in *That's What*) the reforms introduced by Lenin when the communist leader recognised that (to put it bluntly) Soviet Socialism, which

[e] Steve Trafford, *A Cloud in Trousers* (Oberon Books, 2005).

seemed such a good idea and had cost so much in ruined lives and shattered dreams, did not actually work. We may discover here also why the equally unwelcome "reforms" of Stalin's first Five Year Plan (1929), an act of naked authoritarianism, should have supervened destructively upon Mayakovsky's erotic confusion and prompted his suicide in 1930. During the 1920s he had made several trips abroad, including a long visit to America in 1925, which might be interpreted as a hopeless bid to escape from Lily, and where a new love affair climaxed with the birth of his child. Like Hart Crane, Mayakovsky wrote a poem extolling Brooklyn Bridge as the great symbol of modernity and the free human spirit, but he was also deeply troubled by the social inequalities and the racism he found in the America of the time. On his return to the USSR after two years, he wrote the long poem *Khorosho!* (Okay!), a sincere tribute to his communist homeland, while his relationship with Lily continued to form an inexorable counterpoint to everything else, weaving its way through his urbanism, his political commitments and his self-dramatising scrutiny of the creative process. The intensity of the desire formulated in the earlier poem with the Russian title *Lyublyu* – the word for "I love", containing the letters that spell the name of his beloved, Lilya Yurevna Brik – is complemented now by the agonising parables of separation and betrayal of *That's What*.

Lenin's New Economic Policy provided rich material for satire for Mayakovsky as it did for Bulgakov and others. It produced a cavalcade of crooks, hypocrites, speculators and *agents provocateurs*, and its general emphasis on improved living standards gave a new seal of approval to the Soviet *homme moyen sensuel*. Mayakovsky leaped enthusiastically upon this new specimen of humanity and created in his Prisypkin (*The Bedbug*, 1928) a wonderful addition to the gallery of Russian grotesques that began with Gogol early in the nineteenth century and turned into one of the great literary pantheons of all time. The bug-ridden, vodka-soaked Prisypkin is the personification of the vulgarity of the new Soviet man emulating the debauched ways of the bourgeoisie.

At the climax of the play, in an apocalyptic conflagration, firemen's pumped water freezes and Prisypkin with it. He is revived in the utopian society of fifty years later, having lost none of his stupidity and vanity. This "born again" motif, parodied from Christianity, features in a quite startling way in *That's What* as well, in the very specific form of "resurrection" by blood transfusion – one of the (numerous) aberrations of Soviet medical research was the belief that people might be made immortal by this means. The play that followed, *The Bathhouse*, (1930), is a merciless satire on Soviet bureaucracy, with parodies of meaningless socialist jargon that caused great offence. A month after the first performance, Mayakovsky killed himself, playing Russian roulette with a single bullet...

Undoubtedly the reasons for the depression that led to his death were many and various. He had been deeply disturbed and angered by the suicide of the enormously popular poet Sergey Yesenin five years earlier, attributing it to his bohemian lifestyle and alcoholism. The first Five Year Plan, which paved the way for the Great Terror, was no more consistent with Mayakovsky's version of communism than the New Economic Policy had been, and perhaps he despaired now of ever inhabiting the transfigured world of creative desire that he dreamed of. A new love entanglement with a woman in Paris much younger than himself may also have induced despair. But the theme of the poet's suicide, of art as an impassioned dicing with death, of gambling one's life away for the sake of those moments of intensity that banished the nothingness of "byt" (dullness), mere material existence, had haunted Mayakovsky's poetry from the beginning. In *HVM*, he combines Shklovsky's and Tynyanov's Formalism with his own brilliant theses on the political commitment of the poet, illuminating the creative process with a Brechtian trenchancy. The writing is in the spirit of Soviet Constructivism, the art movement that laid bare the formal and material devices of representation, and Mayakovsky's alliance with the brilliant Constructivist Rodchenko came to fruition in the images which were designed to interleave and illuminate the text and which are reproduced here. Rodchenko's inspired photomontages inaugurated a world of new possibilities in combining verbal and visual forms of expression. Mayakovsky's unfinished poem of 1930 entitled *At the Top of My Voice* speaks of "trampling on the throat of his song" in the name of revolutionary politics, but it also reveals a more disciplined kind of imagery than heretofore and an absence of the more extreme kinds of mannerisms. Lenin disliked Mayakovsky's work and called it "hooligan communism" but Stalin, a fellow Georgian, whose own life was steeped in political and personal violence (and whose wife committed suicide in 1932), seems to have valued in Mayakovsky the tenacious, tragic commitment to the ideals of the revolution in the face of all the facts. "Mayakovsky was, and remains, the greatest Soviet poet," he said. Misrepresented in the West, and only half understood, Mayakovsky has nevertheless exerted a powerful influence that has endured to the present, as the remarkable success of Steve Trafford's recent play about his relationship with the Briks confirms. Inevitably, the Mayakovsky industry which flourished in Soviet Russia has gone into a sharp decline, which is on the whole a good thing. However, the debt of some of the best post-war Soviet poets to Mayakovsky's astonishing creativity and impeccable ear for the interplay of speech rhythms and verse rhythms is simply a historical fact.

John Wakeman

TRANSLATING MAYAKOVSKY'S
THAT'S WHAT

Translating Mayakovsky isn't easy. At different times, translators have taken very different angles on him. This is perhaps the case with any major writer, but not always to this extreme degree. One intractable problem for his readers and translators has always been the amount of openly propagandist writing in his work. His propaganda is often brilliantly inventive in linguistic terms, and even very witty and engaging. Invariably it is more than propaganda, being linked to a complex drama of identity. But still it may be hard for all but committed communists to swallow. For a long time the intensely political translations of his verse by Herbert Marshall held sway and English readers knew Mayakovsky mainly as Stalin's Party laureate, the First Poet of Socialism. But Boris Pasternak, who greatly admired Mayakovsky, and learned from his astonishing technical virtuosity and profound understanding of the Russian language, remarked on the way his poetry had been imposed by force on the Soviet people "like potatoes under Catherine the Great".*f* His suicide in 1930, which the Party accounted for in terms of the kind of personal problems *That's What* narrates, somehow did not impinge much upon the official hagiography, because he was felt to be such a "good thing", in a nation with such a high regard for its poets, that his iconic status would surely outlive his untidy life, with a little help from his friends. "This was his second death", said Pasternak, "he had had no part in it."*g* There was no need, apparently, to attribute his growing depression, which led to his suicide, to the brutal hijacking of the revolution he loved and the violent political transformation of the Soviet Union that came with the first Five Year Plan at the end of the permissive '20s. The year 1929 marked the end of the era of phoney compromise in which the Communist Party tried to cover up the radical failures of the system by means of the kinds of market-led reforms that Mayakovsky

f Boris Pasternak, *Safe Conduct* (New Directions, 1958).
g *ibid.*

pours scorn on in the poem translated here, as Bulgakov does in *The Master and Margarita*. What followed under Stalin was a much more systematic assault on the "traitors" and "saboteurs" who had brought about the humiliating failures of The System. Mayakovsky's personal fusion of revolutionary idealism with Modernist poetics exploits the cultural instability of the historical state of affairs in the '20s with wonderful *élan*. After the early '20s it was no longer needed, and it was not likely to survive what came next.

A later translator, Edwin Morgan, making effective use of a synthetic variety of "lallans Scots" (essentially a synthesis of the language of Burns and the celebrated Jamieson dictionary)[h] very effectively, gives Mayakovsky a suitably dissident and popular voice, with the inventive poetic dialect providing the right kind of linguistic "strangeness", and allowing for all sorts of experiment-alism and neologisms, like Mayakovsky's own work. Yet with Mayakovsky, as the poet said himself, love, the ultimate defamil-iarising experience we can all share in, was "the heart of everything." Crossing the boundaries of the real, the imaginary and the symbolic in the name of desire is his "everything" and his experiments are, like Eliot's, calculated to "dislocate language into meaning"[j] under the pressure of urgent personal experience, not intrinsically for effect or even in the service of any political agenda. As with Eliot's *The Love Song of J. Alfred Prufrock*, with which Mayakovsky's poem has a strange kinship, the richly figurative language gives rise to an endless series of erotic defamiliarisations, the "making strange" of his friend Viktor Shklovsky,[k] in which

[h] John Jamieson's *Dictionary of the Scottish Language* was first published in Edinburgh in 1808. The "Scottish" it is concerned with is not Gaelic but a highly-developed variant of English. Reprinted in an abridged version, this book influenced Scottish writers enormously.
[j] T. S. Eliot, *The Metaphysical Poets*, 1921.
[k] Victor Shklovsky, *Art as Device*, 1917, translated as *Art as Technique* in Lemon and Reis, eds., *Russian Formalist Criticism Four Essays*, (University of Nebraska, 1965).

15

the poetic persona, or "lyrical self", is split metonymically and metaphorically by the self-contradictory intensity of the need for love and the simultaneous fear of intimacy and self-abandonment. The present translators have taken the poem's title, which in Russian is *Pro Eto*, meaning literally "about this thing", and rendered it by the more defiant, take-it-or-leave-it "that's what", in the hope of conveying a sense of the defiant conjunction of desire and dread that the poem contains. The relationship with Lily Brik, which gave birth to these contradictory feelings, is dramatised in this poem, more than in any other Mayakovsky poem, in all its neurotic splendour. Mayakovsky's very title contains the already explosive potential for "yoking together heterogeneous ideas" (another phrase from Eliot)[l] typical of his modernist sensibility, and reinforced in the witty and exuberant photo-montages Rodchenko supplied to "illustrate" the fragmented, enigmatic text like some sort of supercharged machine-age choreography. The minimal Russian words of the title, a sort of bureau-cratic jargon, also evoke the word "poet" and the word "proletarian"; and the text is indeed concerned with how poems get written and the nature of class consciousness, in the context of the trials and tribulations of maintaining his intimate relationship with his muse / lover under increasingly difficult conditions, virtually a sort of Party surveillance. But my theme is...

And the significance of that (suppressed) "that" surely cannot be overestimated. "That", the unnameable, was what made Mayakovsky tick. "That" was "what" the authorities air-brushed out of photographs,[m] the personal intimacy that had taken on epic proportions, bracketing Lily, the wife of a Formalist theorist, Osip, with the "decadence" Mayakovsky "ought" to have left behind with his yellow Futurist waistcoat, the symbol of Bohemianism.

---

[l] Dr. Johnson's observation about the seventeenth-century poet Cowley was applied by Eliot, Leavis and other proponents of a modern style in poetry.
[m] cf. Bengt Jangfeldt, *Love in the Heart of Everything*, Grove, 1987.

"Formalist" was already becoming a dirty word. Lily Brik's husband had been cast by the new puritans in some kind of quasi-demonic role, seducer of the Soviet bard into some sort of avant-garde sexual experiment (which existed mostly in their overheated imaginations). The supercharged neologisms of Mayakovsky's verse cover an immense lexical and grammatical range as they trace the events of 1922, which the indispensable Bengt Jangfeldt tells us " was a crisis year in the tripartite relationship involving Mayakovsky, Lily, and Osip. But there was nothing intrinsically lurid about it. Lily had been in Riga, where British visas were obtainable, on her way to see her sister Elsa in London and had lingered in the hope of getting some Mayakovsky texts published. But the decision to live apart for a while came (characteristically) from the sense they both had, while living together in Berlin, that their intimacy was threatened by the "byt" condemned by Mayakovsky in his suicide poem ("byt" is a very Russian concept of dullness, meaning "everyday life", "the commonplace", "the familiar"). For the arch-Romantic Mayakovsky, there was no possible reconciliation between the transfiguring intensity of his desire, a mad sort of ego-mania, and day-to-day "married" life. The "defamiliarising" games with language in *That's What* stem, like the game of Russian Roulette which ended Maya-kovsky's life, from the torment of an unendurable separation posited upon an impossible intimacy. A wild dream logic organises them. As Jangfeldt tells us, during this time (a period of two months) Mayakovsky did not visit Lily once.

> But he went up to her house, hid on the staircase, crept up to the doors of her flat and wrote her letters and notes, which were handed to her by the servants or by mutual friends; he sent her flowers, books, and other presents... A few times they met by chance...[p]

That's What tells this story, in its own way, through Mayakovsky's

[n] Jangfeldt, *op. cit.*
[p] Jangfeldt, *op. cit.*

epic urban metaphors and Rodchenko's photomontages, which run parallel and open up ever new figurative perspectives on life-events, sometimes taking traditional *topoi* of landscape and legend as starting points.

"Take breath and read it with your ears", as Hopkins advised Bridges, [q] in relation to his own poetry, and many of the difficulties disappear. There is an excellent prose paraphrase of *Pro Eto* in the Charters's fine study of Mayakovsky called *I Love*. [r] But the translator / reader still needs to leap from rock to rock, the way Mayakovsky did when expounding his own version of "sprung rhythm". [s] Or as he says in *HVM* [t] "you" (for reader and writer are in some sense one) listen for that "dull roar" that issues from time to time in sounds that turn into the words which keep searching for meanings. It's like being at the dentist and having a tooth crowned, he says in *HVM* – a painful quest for a good fit. It's also like Christmas, when many pasts and presents fuse in the nightmare of ritual self-abandonment called "the family". The poet, caught between self-dramatisation and self-abasement, inserts a rather desperate allusion to Oscar Wilde as another victim of a "love that dare not speak its name". Scattering neologisms of all sorts, from Soviet jargon to the cries of street urchins, Mayakovsky struggles to make words fit the almost incommunicable love he feels for Lily, which transcends "byt". A phone-call to her becomes a helpless encounter with the troglodytic backwardness of Moscow, waiting to be banished by the Revolution, and for the poet maybe a battle to the death with Fate as well. People have been killed by lightning striking telephones: and in Russian an Express telegram was "molniya", a lightning flash. But the overall impression here is of the cumbersome slowness of Moscow, resisting the poet's passionate declamation. As inarticulate as a bear, as he tells us, he floats helplessly away on

[q] *The Letters of Gerard Manley Hopkins to Robert Bridges* (OUP, 1935).
[r] A. and S. Charters, *I Love* (Andre Deutsch, 1967).
[s] *cf.* Jangfeldt, *op. cit.*
[t] *HVM, op. cit.*

an ice-flow borne along by the tide of his tears. The metonymic, Cubist splitting of signifier and signified, word and image, texture and substance, reproduced in Rodchenko's witty photomontages, constructs contradictory angles on events, a visual / verbal "dialectic" indeed, and keeps generating new metaphors: the bear, the ice-flow, the open sea, are at the same time the poet, his bed, a suitcase and a fireplace, all loosened from their moorings. As language splits, so does the Mayakovsky-persona, the bard of the Revolution and the Wildean victim of a "forbidden" love that could not speak its name in a language acceptable to the inhabitants of "byt".

The fact that it is Christmas, when lonely people traditionally top themselves and everybody overspends, allows Mayakovsky to step sideways into imagery already evoked by Blok (in his poem 'The Twelve') yoking together Christ and the Revolution under a forlorn sign of Redemption or Deliverance (even such a good Victorian as Matthew Arnold thought that finding "deliverance", setting the spirit free in a new language, was the poet's real job). A young Komsomolets (a member of the Communist Youth movement) stands in for Christ, taking Blok's imagery one step further but, like Mayakovsky, he is in a suicidal state of mind from thwarted love. Volodya's family, with a great outpouring of domestic chatter, await him with their Merry X Certificate celebrations, from which he instantly counts himself out – only to be excluded all over again, this time from Lily's entourage, as he stands playing a spectral card game with the windowpanes of her apartment (hoping for a glimpse of her as a gambler hopes for his "deliverance"). Echoes of Dostoevsky (the guilty drama of the stairs in *Crime and Punishment*) enfold an Eliotesque (as in *Prufrock*) lament for love locked out. Just how bawdy or licentious her gathering really is we can only guess; we only know his lurid fantasies as he "cut out patterns from the shouted words" of her guests, who seem to be mocking him. As with Eliot's *Prufrock*, the poet's language (and therefore that of the translator) shifts between literary and non-literary idioms. Poems and sacred texts, execrations and endearments, and above all infinite self-conscious self-analysis, "dislocate" words into meaning, as Eliot said the modern poet must, fitting a changed expression to a changed sensibility. And beneath and within it all is the insecure "love song" of a man who wants too much, though he does not know what, from the obscure object of his desire, who (when it comes down to it) does not really know what he wants or means, much as she likes him.

Pro Eto ends with a strange kind of apotheosis. The suicidal "man on the bridge", who is one version of Mayakovsky, might just be resurrected, he thinks, as someone who could live placidly in the "real" world. His best bet, he thinks, might be to be reincarnated as a zoo-keeper, because he knows Lily loves animals as much as he does; one day while visiting the zoo she might just stray into his terrain. Appropriately enough, Soviet medical science had already begun to address the problem of eternal life / resurrection, promising something of the sort through blood transfusions which were supposed to function like some kind of early cryogenics and keep people going more or less for ever. [u] The Formalists spoke of the "resurrection of the word" [v] and Jakobson and Shklovsky saw in Futurism not just a new aesthetic principle but a transformation of consciousness equivalent to an apocalyptic vision of a new world. With Mayakovsky, too, Christian imagery is never far away, fuelling his creative use of blasphemy, often applied to the Revolution. The poet is both Christ and Antichrist. The cross Mayakovsky bears links him with Pasternak and even with Pasternak's Soviet anti-hero, Dr. Zhivago, who also carried throughout his life the cross of his conviction that love was "the heart of everything", and interpreted the Revolution as a daemonic kind of "deliverance". It was specifically love's boat that was wrecked, in Mayakovsky's farewell poem, against

---

[u] Alexander Bogdanov (1873-1029) wrote important science fiction as a sideline to his other careers as an exponent of systems thinking and biology. The idea that blood transfusion might rejuvenate is nicely debunked in William Empson's poem 'Missing Dates'.

[v] Viktor Shklovsky, *The Resurrection of the Word*, 1914.

the rocks of "byt".

This translation follows Mayakovsky in the way he followed Lily, obsessively but not always faithfully. The poet works across and against the constraints of Russian syntax and poetics, but there are some boundaries of rectitude he cannot, or will not, demolish. Listening to another, related rhetoric, that of the "beat" poet and the rock musician, the translators sometimes storm the barricade of language and propriety, in the name of the new perspective Mayakovsky and Rodchenko and their brilliant contemporaries opened up.

George Hyde

ПРО ЧТО – ПРО ЭТО?

В этой теме
       и личной
        и мелкой
перепетой не раз
        и не пять
я кружил поэтической белкой
и хочу кружиться опять.
Эта тема
      сейчас
          и молитвой у Будды
и у негра вострит на хозяев нож.
Если Марс
      и на нем хоть один сердцелюдый,
то и он
      сейчас
      скрипит
        про то-ж.
Эта тема придет
      калеку за локти
подтолкнет к бумаге
       прикажет:
         скреби!
И калека
     с бумаги
       срывается в клёкоте
только строчками в солнце песня рябит.
Эта тема придет,
     позвонится с кухни,
повернется,

*Liberate perception from automism, key to
formalist russian poetry / defamiliarisation*

WHAT'S THIS? – THAT'S WHAT

This theme,
      repeated quite a few times,
            is a poor thing, but my own;
a squirrel's cage where
      I go round and round
          feeling more and more alone
praying for it not to stop
      like a Buddhist monk
         turning his prayer wheel
or like a black guy
      carving "I love you"
         on his neighbour's skin.
If the planet Mars
      has just one humanoid
         inhabitant,
then he as well
      will squeak out the same tune,
         and his din
will sound
      very much
        like my rant.
Along comes this theme
      takes the limping poet
         by the arm
plonks him down
      with paper and pen
         till soon he's getting warm
scraping away
      till the sunbeams shine
         from out his lines.
This theme
      echoes from the kitchen
         like a bell from the maid's room,
pirouettes
      and crumbles

23

Mina Lloyd

сгинет шапченкой гриба –
и гигант
       постоит секунду
                и рухнет
под записочной рябью себя погребя.
Эта тема придет
       прикажет:
           – Истина! –
Эта тема придет
       велит:
           – Красота! –
И пускай
       перекладиной кисти раскистены
только вальс под нос мурлычешь с креста.
Эта тема азбуку тронет разбегом –
уж на что б казалось книга ясна? –
и становится
            – А –
               недоступней Казбека.
Замутит
       оттянет от хлеба и сна.
Эта тема придет,
       вовек не износится, –
только скажет:
       отныне гляди на меня!
И глядишь на нее
       и идешь знаменосцем
красношелкий огонь над землей знаменя.

like a mushroom –
like some big guy who
           struts for a moment while
                a sunbeam lights his way to dusty
                        death.
Along comes this theme which
                demands no less than
                    truth.
Along comes this theme which
                demands no less than
                    beauty.
Paintbrushes lose their fur
                artists their sense of balance
but you hum a furtive waltz tune
                crucified by your torments.
This theme
        flips through the alphabet
                at the double –
how did writing
          ever get to look
              such child's play? –
the letter
    'A'
          is harder to get to than the Caucasus.[1]
It makes you ill
          drags you from your nosh and your kip.
Along comes this theme
              eternally bloody inexhaustible
and tells you:
         Just look at me! for ever and a day!
So you can't take your eyes off it
               you carry a flag for it
a red silk flame
         bannering
            across the planet

Это хитрая тема!

     Нырнет под событья,
в тайниках инстинктов готовясь к прыжку, –
и как будто ярясь

    – посмели забыть ее! –
затрясет;

      посыпятся души из шкур.
Эта тема ко мне заявилась гневная,
приказала:

    – Подать

       дней удила!
Посмотрела скривясь в мое ежедневное
и грозой раскидала людей и дела.
Эта тема пришла,

     остальные оттерла
и одна

      безраздельно стала близка.
Эта тема ножом подступила к горлу
Молотобоец!

     от сердца к вискам.
Эта тема день истемнила в темень,

and it gets its cunning claws
                    into you,
burrows deep down
                    under things.
In secret places
                    of instinct
                              it gets ready to spring
sort of raging:
                    – do you dare to forget that?
                                        – be a man!
shaking your
                    soul out of
                              its skin.
The theme
                    came to me
                              enraged, demanding:
Grab time by the nose!
Took a sideways
                    look
                              at my daily grind
scattered people
                    and things
                              like a cloudburst.
Along came this theme
                    shoving everything else aside
and just one thing
                    stayed put
                              immovable.
This theme
          held a knife to my throat, like
some blacksmith's apprentice
                    hammering a rhythm from heart to temples above.
This theme
                    turned daylight
                              to darkness,

колотись – велела – строчками
лбов.
Имя
    этой
        теме:

                ......!

I. БАЛЛАДА РЕДИНГСКОЙ ТЮРЬМЫ

> *Стоял – вспоминаю.*
> *Был этот блеск.*
> *И это,*
> *тогда,*
> *называлось Невою.*
> Маяковский. „Человек".
> (13 лет работы, II т., стр. 77)

О балладе   Не молод очень лад баллад, –
и о   но если слова болят
балладах.   и слова говорят про то что болят
              молодеет и лад баллад.
              Лубянский проезд.
                    Водопьяный.
                      Вид
    вот.
        Вот
            фон.
В постели она.
      Она лежит.
Он.
На столе телефон.
„Он" и „она" баллада моя.
Не страшно новая.

hammered home
                    lines
                                   into my forehead.
The name
            of the theme
                              is……

1. THE BALLAD OF READING GAOL

I was standing, I remember.
There was a gleam of light.
So that,
then,
was the River Neva [2]
                              Mayakovsky 'Man'

On the ballad   The music of the ballad sure ain't new –
and on   but if its words are words of pain
ballads.   and its words describe the pain again
                    the ballad too renews its old refrain.
                    Lubyansky passage.[3]
                        Vodopyany.[4]
                                It looked
                    like this.
                              Over there
                                        the background.
                    She lies
                          in bed.
                    While he…
                    On the table is a telephone.
                    "He" and "she" are my ballad.
                    Not terribly original you say.

В постели она.
Она лежит.
Он.
На столе телефон.

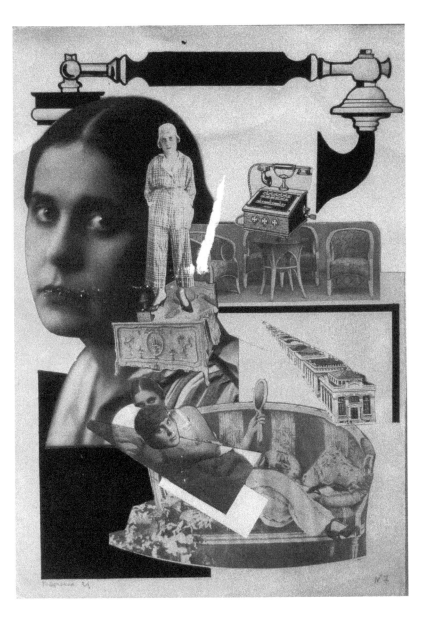

She lies
    in bed.
While he…
On the table is a telephone.

Страшно то
    что „он" это я
и то что „она" –
      моя.
При чем тюрьма?
    Рождество.
      Кутерьма.
Без решеток окошки домика!
Это вас не касается.
    Говорю – тюрьма.
Стол.
    На столе соломинка.

По кабелю Тронул еле – волдырь на теле.
пущен номер.   Трубку из рук вон.
Из фабричной марки – две стрелки яркие
           омолниили телефон.
Соседняя комната.
    Из соседней
      сонно:
Когда это?
    откуда это живой поросенок?
Звонок от ожогов уже визжит;
добела раскален аппарат.
Больна она!
    Она лежит!
Беги!
    Скорей!
      Пора!
Мясом дымясь, сжимаю жжение.
Моментально молния телом забегала.
Стиснул миллион вольт напряжения.

Terrible though
that "he" is me
and that "she"
is mine.
So why this jail?
Christmas.
Bustle.
The little house's windows have no bars.
But that's immaterial.
It's a gaol I tell you.
A table.
On the table
straw.
I just touched it –
look at the burn mark

The phone line accepts a call. The handset leaped from my hand.
From the trademark – two bright arrows
turned the phone to lightning.
The next room…
From the next room
a sleepy voice:
"When is it?
Where's this bloody piglet come from?"
The telephone bell is screaming from its burns;
the phone is white-hot.
She's ill!
Sick in bed!
Run!
Faster!
Double-quick!
My flesh smokes as I grip the burning
A flash of lightning ran through my body on the instant
clenched by a million volt current.

Ткнулся губой в телефонное пекло.
Дыры
    сверля
        в доме,
взмыв
    Мясницкую
        пашней,
рвя
  кабель,
     номер
пулей
  летел
     барышне.
Смотрел осовело барышнин глаз,
под праздник работай за двух. –
Красная лампа опять зажглась.
Позвонила!
   огонь потух.
И вдруг
    как по лампам пошло куралесить,
вся сеть телефонная рвется на нити. –
67-10!
Соедините!
В проулок!
  Скорей!
      Водопьяному в тишь!
Ух!
  А то с электричеством станется –
под Рождество
  на воздух взлетишь –
со всей
  со своей

I thrust my lips into the telephone hell
screwing holes
                    through
                              the house,
soaring over
          the ploughlands of
                              Myasnitskaya,[5]
lacerating
          the wires,
                    the number
sped
     like a bullet
                    towards her ladyship.
Looked dazedly into her ladyship's eyes:
"Before the holiday work twice as hard."
The little red light is glowing again.
It's her ringing!
                    The fire dies down
and suddenly
               as if ricocheting
                              from valve to valve
the whole network
                    is torn into shreds.
67-10!
Connect!
Down the sidestreet!
                    Quick!
                              Vodopyany
is silent as the dead.
Ouf!
    And what will become of the electrics –
at Christmas too –
                    you'll be blown sky-high
and everything
          all of its

35

телефонной
станцией.
Жил на Мясницкой один старожил.
Сто лет после этого жил –
про это лишь –
сто лет! –
говаривал детям дед.
Было – суббота…
под воскресенье…
Окорочек…
Хочу, чтоб дешево…
Как вдарит кто-то!…
Землетресенье…
Ноге горячо…
Ходун – подошва!…
Не верилось детям,
чтоб так-то
да там-то.
Землетресенье?
Зимой?
У почтамта?!

Телефон бросается на всех. Протиснувшись чудом сквозь тоненький шнур
раструба трубки разинув оправу,
погромом звонков громя тишину
разверг телефон дребезжащую лаву.
Это визжащее,
звенящее это, –
пальнуло в стены,
старалось взорвать их.
Звоночинки
тыщей
от стен
рикошетом

                                     local switchboards.
An old boy once lived on Myasnitskaya.
A hundred years after this moment
– this theme will last at least a hundred years! –
this grandad was chatting to the kids.
It was Saturday…
                                     Sunday coming
A nice leg – of chicken?
                                     Just the job,
                                             not too dear…

Will someone
                     give me one?…
                                             An earthquake…
It makes my foot burn…
                                     tottering – my bootsole…
The kids wouldn't believe it,
                                     that this way
                                             and there.

An earthquake?
                     In winter?
                                             At the post office?!
The   Squeezing miraculously
telephone   through the thin wire,
throws itself   stretching the rim
at everyone.   of the mouthpiece funnel,
                       a thunder of ringings
                                             bangs through the silence,
                       then the telephone pours out its tinkling lava.
A screaming,
                     a ringing,
shots slammed into the wall
                                             tried to blow it up.
Thousands
                     of bell-lets
                                     ricocheted

37

под стулья закатывались
                      и под кровати.
Об пол с потолка звоночище хлопал.
И снова
        звенящий мячище точно
взлетал к потолку ударившись об пол
и сыпало вниз дребезгою звоночной.
Стекло за стеклом
              вьюшку за вьюшкой
тянуло
        звенеть телефонному в тон.
Тряся
      рученочкой
            дом погремушку
тонул в разливе звонков телефон.

Сенундантша. От сна.
                  чуть видно –
                        точка глаз –
иголит щеки жаркие.
Ленясь кухарка поднялась
идет
        кряхтя и харкая.
Мочёном яблокам она.
Морщинят мысли лоб ее.
Кого?
Владим Владимыч?!
А!
Пошла туфлею шлепая.
Идет.
Отмеряет шаги секундантом.
Шаги отдаляются…
        Слышатся еле…
Весь мир остальной отодвинут куда-то
лишь трубкой в меня неизвестное целит.

                        from the wall
rolling under the chairs
                    and under the bed.
From the ceiling a great bell banged out.
And then again
                a ringing sphere sort of flew
to the ceiling, banging against the floor,
sprinkling down a tinkle of bells.
Window pane after pane
                            the stove's metal doors
rang out with a ringing
                        like a host of phones.
The house
        shaken like a child's rattle
                            in a tiny hand
drowned in the gulf of telephone bells.

The second.   From sleep
            scarcely visible
                        a dotted eye
needle-eye in hot cheeks.
The cook lazily rises
and goes
            mumbling and coughing.
She looks like a cider apple
with thoughts wrinkling her brow.
"Who?
            Vladimir Vladimirovich?!
                            Ah!"
Off she shuffles in her slippers
measuring her paces
                    like a second in a duel.
Her steps grow distant…
                    You can hardly hear them…
The rest of the world has gone away somewhere
the unknown is aiming its receiver at me.

Просветление мира. Застыли докладчики всех заседаний,
не могут закончить начатый жест.
Как были,
      рот разинув
            сюда они
смотрят на Рождество из Рождеств.
Им видима жизнь
      от дрязг и до дрязг.
Дом их
      единая будняя тина
Будто в себя
      в меня смотрясь
ждали
      смертельной любви поединок.
Окаменели сиренные рокоты.
      Колес и шагов суматоха не вертит.
Лишь поле дуэли
      да время доктор
с бескрайним бинтом исцеляющей смерти.
Москва –
      за Москвой поля примолкли.
Моря –
      за морями горы стройны.
Вселенная
            вся
            как будто в бинокле
в огромном бинокле (с другой стороны).

The world enlightened. Delegates freeze in mid-conference,
they break off in mid-gesture.
Opened-mouthed,
                    caught in the act
                                        they advance
gaping at the Christmas
                    to end all Christmases.
These people see life whole
                    from squabble to squabble,
Their home is
            life's workaday slime.
Maybe looking into
                    my face
                                like a mirror
what they want
            is a duel
                    a deadly love to the death.
Petrified
        are the rumbling sirens.
The bustle
        of wheels and footsteps
                                    immobilised.
Only
        this duelling place
                                with time the doctor
with his endless bandage of healing death.
Moscow –
        and outside of Moscow the fields fall silent.
Oceans –
        beyond the oceans mountains are levelled.
The entire universe
                    seen
                            through giant binoculars
binoculars

41

Горизонт распрямился
    ровно ровно.
Тесьма.
    Натянут бичевкой тугой.
Край один:
    я в моей комнате, –
ты в своей комнате край другой.
А между
    такая,
      какая не снится, –
какая-то гордая белой обновой
через вселенную
    легла Мясницкая
миниатюрой кости слоновой.
Ясность.
    Прозрачнейшей ясностью пытка.
В Мясницкой
    деталью искуснейшей щеточки
кабель
    тонюсенький –
      ну, просто нитка!
И все
    вот на этой вот держится ниточке.

Дуэль. Раз!
Трубку наводят.
    Надежду
брось.
    Два!
    Как раз
остановилась
    не дрогнув

turned back to front.
The horizon
gradually grows flat.
A ribbon
drawn tight as a rope.
One end of it:
that's me in my room,
you in your room is the other end.
In between
undreamed-of
Myasnitskaya
in full view
of the universe
looking sort of
proud of her new white dress,
a miniature
carved in ivory.
Clarity
more translucent than under torture.
On Myasnitskaya
one fine-drawn detail shows
artfully,
a cable
most slender –
really no more than a thread –
and everything
hangs on this little thread.

The duel. One!
They aim the receiver.
Abandon
hope.
Two!
Poised
precisely
without trembling

между

моих

мольбой обволокнутых глаз.
Хочется крикнуть медлительной бабе, –
Чего задаетесь?

Стоите Дантесом.
Скорей

скорей просверлите сквозь кабель
нулей

любого яда и веса.
Страшнее пуль

оттуда

сюда вот
кухаркой оброненное между зевот
проглоченным кроликом в брюхе удава
по кабелю

вижу

слово ползет.
Страшнее слов

из древнейшей древности
где самку клыком добывали люди еще
ползло

из шнура –

скребущейся ревности
времен трогладитских тогдашнее чудище.
А может быть…

Наверное может!
Никто в телефон не лез и не лезет, –
нет никакой трогладйчьей рожи.
Сам в телефоне.

                                    between
my entreating eyes.
I want to scream
                        at the dawdling woman, –
Why do you play games?
                        You stand like Danthes.[6]
Faster
      drill faster through the cable,
bullets
         never mind how heavy and poisonous.
More terrible
            than the bullet
                        between there and here
dropped by the cook between yawns
                                    I see
like a swallowed rabbit
                        in a python's belly
crawling
         along the wire
                     a word.
More terrible than the words
                        of ancient antiquity
when men
         fought for women
                     with their bare fangs,
from the cable
            crawled –
scratching jealously –
                     a monster from troglodytic
                                              times.
And can this be…
                 it seems as if it can!
No-one has climbed (nor ever will) into the phone,
there's no troglodyte's mug.
It's me, mirrored

Ползло
    из шнура –
        скребущейся ревности
времен трогладитских тогдашнее чудище.

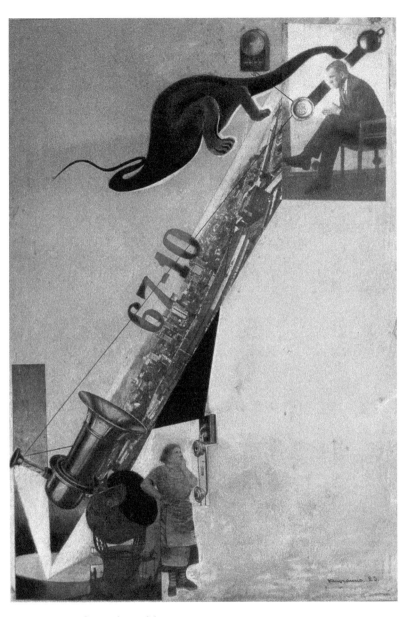

from the cable
       crawled –
scratching jealously –
           a monster from troglodytic times.

Зеркалюсь в железе.
Возьми и пиши ему ВЦИК циркуляры!
Пойди – эту правильность с Эрфуртской сверь:
Сквозь первое горе
            бессмысленный
                 ярый
мозг поборов
          проскребается зверь.

Что может сдедаться с человеком? Красивый вид.
      Товарищи!
      Взвесьте!
В Париж гастролировать едущий летом поэт.
Почтенный   сотрудник Известий
царапает стул когтем из штиблета.
Вчера человек
      единым махом
клыками свой размедведил вид я!
Косматый.
     Шерстью свисает рубаха.
Тоже туда-ж!?
     В телефоны бабахать!?
К своим пошел!
     В моря ледовитые!

in the phone's iron.

Grab him,

send him some memos

from the

All-Union Executive Committee.[7]

Go and check

his political correctness

by the light

of the Erfurt Programme.[8]

A beast scratches its way

senseless

with rage

through first

grief,

brain heavy

with defeat.

What can hap- What a lovely spectacle.
pen to a   Comrades!
man?   Take stock!

A poet makes a summer trip to Paris.

The honoured co-worker of *Izvestiya*[9]

scratches a chair

with his smart winkle-picker

like a claw.

Yesterday one man

– me –

with one snap of his

fangs

turned into a bear.

Hairy

pelt flopping like a loose shirt.

ARE YOU TRYING TO GET IN THERE TOO??!

Booming into telephones like that!?

Go join your own kith and kin

on the icy seas!

49

Размедвеж-
енье.

Медведем
      когда он смертельно сердится
на телефон
    грудь
       на врага тяну.
А сердце·
      глубже уходит в рогатину!
Течет.
      Ручьища красной меди.
Рычанье и кровь.
      Лакай темнота!
Не знаю
    плачут ли
      нет медведи
но если плачут
      то именно так.
То именно так:
      без сочувственной фальши
скулят
      заливаясь ущельной длиной.
И именно так их медвежий Бальшин
скуленьем разбужен ворчит за стеной.
Вот так медведи именно могут:
недвижно
    задравши морду
        как те
повыть
    извыться
      и лечь в берлогу
царапая логово в двадцать когтей.
Сорвался лист.
    Обвал.
        Беспокоит.
Винтовки шишки
    не грохнули б враз.

Turning
beary
all over.

The bear
    when he's really very shirty on the phone
bares his breast
        to the foe, toe-to-toe
While his heart
      drives deeper into his mighty
           hunting-horn!
Time passes.
      A mighty stream of red bronze,
round my roaring blood.
          Lap, waves of darkness.
I do not know if bears
       weep
but if they weep
      they weep like this.
Just like this:
      not putting it on at all
they whimper
      flooding the length and breadth
        of their cave.
And their beary neighbour, Balshin,
      upset by the whimpering,
        growls
behind the wall.
You see what a bear can do actually:
motionless,
      his snout turned skyward
he can whine, bear-like,
      to the last whine
        then just lie down
in his beary lair
scrabbling with his twenty claws.
A leaf falls.
    Like an avalanche.
        It disturbs him.

Ему лишь взмедведиться может такое
сквозь слезы и шерсть бахромящую глаз

Протекающая Кровать
комната.
⠀⠀⠀Железки
⠀⠀⠀⠀⠀Брахло одеяло.
Лежит в железках
⠀⠀⠀Тихо
⠀⠀⠀⠀⠀Вяло.
Трепет пришел.
⠀⠀⠀Пошел по железкам.
Простынь постельная треплется плеском.
Вода лизнула холодом ногу.
Откуда вода?
⠀⠀⠀Почему много?
Сам наплакал
⠀⠀⠀Плакса
⠀⠀⠀⠀⠀Слякоть.
Неправда –
⠀⠀⠀Столько нельзя наплакать.
Чортова ванна!
⠀⠀⠀вода за диваном.
Под столом
⠀⠀⠀за шкафом вода.
С дивана,
⠀⠀⠀сдвинут воды задеваньем
в окно проплыл чемодан.
Камин
⠀⠀⠀Окурок
⠀⠀⠀⠀⠀Сам кинул
Пойти потушить
⠀⠀⠀Петушится
⠀⠀⠀⠀⠀Страх.

Falling pinecones thud at intervals like bullets.
All this penetrates his beary senses only
   through tears and the furry fringes
      of his eyes.

**The room
leaks.**
 A bed,
   iron frame
     rags of blankets.
He lies on his iron frame
    limply
      floppily.

A tremor starts
    spreading through the iron bars.
The bed-linen waves and splashes
Water licks coldly at his feet
Where does it come from?
     Why so much of it?

He wept buckets
    cry-baby
      slush-puppy
Can't be true –
    you just can't weep that much.
A bloody great bath-full!
     Water behind the settee
Under the table
    Water behind the cupboard.
From the settee,
    carried by the surge of water
out of the window
    floats
     a suitcase.
In the fireplace
   A fag-end
     I threw it there myself
Go and put it out
    Make a show of defiance

Куда?

К какому такому камину?
Верста,

За верстою берег в кострах.
Размыло все

даже запах капустный
с кухни

всегдашний

приторно сладкий.
Река.

Вдали берега.

Как пусто!
Как ветер воет в догонку с Ладоги!
Река.

Большая река.

Холодина.
Рябит река.

Я в середине.
Белым медведем

взлез на льдину

плыву на своей
подушке льдине.
Бегут берега

за видом вид.
Подо мной подушки лед.
С Ладоги дует

вода бежит.
Летит подушка плот.
Плыву.

Лихоражуеь на льдине подушке.
Одно ощущенье водой не вымыто:—
Я должен

не то под кроватные дужки

                        Terrified!

Where?

    Where the hell is the fireplace?

Miles away.

           See the bonfires on the distant shore.

Everything washed out,

                  even the smell of cabbage

from the kitchen

            everlastingly

                  cloyingly sweet.

A river.

      The shores are far off.

                     How empty it is!

How the wind howls at your back

                from Lake Ladoga![10]

A river.

      A huge river.

             Bitterly cold.

A glittering river

           and me in the middle.

A white bear

           stuck on an ice-floe

           floating on my icy pillow.

The shores pass by

             scene after scene.

Beneath my pillow, ice.

The wind from Ladoga,

              the water runs.

The pillow raft flies.

I am sailing.

            I am feverish on my ice pillow.

The only sensation

             not washed out by the water is –

I must either sail under

              the ridged edge of the bed

ие то

        под мостом проплыть под каким-то.
Были вот так же

        ветер да я.
Эта река!…

    Не эта

       Иная.
Нет не иная!

       Было:

        Стоял.
Было – блестело

    теперь вспоминаю.
Мысль растет.

     Не справлюсь я с нею.
Назад!

     Вода не выпустит плот.
Видней и видней…

     Ясней и яснее…
Теперь неизбежно…

    Он будет!

    Он вот!!!

Человек из-за 7-ми лет. Волны устои стальные моют.
Недвижный

     страшный

        упершись в бока
столицы

   в отчаяньи созданной мною
стоит

    на своих стоэтажных быках.
Небо воздушными скрепами вышил.
Из вод феерией стали восстал.
Глаза подымаю выше

        выше…
Вон!

   Вон –

or under
         some sort of a bridge.
It was just like this, just the two of us
                  the wind and I.
The river!…
        No, not this one,
               Another.
No, not another!
         And that's how
              I stood.
And so – it shone
         as I remember.
My thoughts expand
          I cannot cope with them.
Back!
     The water won't give up the raft.
It's more and more obvious…
            Clearer and clearer.
By now ineluctable…
        Here he comes!
            Here he is!

The same Waves wash the steel pillars.
man seven Motionless I am
years on.   terrible
         hands on hips
A capital city
      I founded on my despair
A bridge? It stands
       on its hundred-storey foundations.
Embroidering heaven with its airy girders.
Fairy towers of steel rise from the waves.
I lift my eyes higher
       higher…
See there!
    Over there –

опершись о перила моста...
Прости Нева!
    Не прощает,
        гонит.
Сжалься!
    Не сжалился бешеный бег.
Он!
    Он –

        у небес в воспаленном фоне
прикрученный мною стоит человек.
Стоит.
    Разметал изросшие волосы.
Я уши лаплю.
    Напрасные мнешь!
Я слышу
        мой
            мой собственный голос.
Мне лапы дырявит голоса нож.
Мой собственный голос –
        он молит –
        он просится:
Владимир!
    Остановись!
        Не покинь!
Зачем ты тогда не позволил мне броситься!
С размаху сердце разбить о быки?
Семь лет я стою.
    Я смотрю в эти воды
к перилам прикручен канатами строк.
Семь лет с меня глаз эти воды не сводят.

          leaning on the rails of the bridge…
Neva, forgive us!
          It won't forgive,
               it drives us away.
Have mercy on us!
        This demonic fugue is remorseless.
Him!
    He –
        silhouetted against the feverish sky
this man stands
        clamped by me
            to the rails.
His shaggy hair
        flows on the wind.
I paw at
     my ears
        kneading uselessly.
I hear
    my own
       my very own voice.
The knife
     of this voice bores through
              my paws.
My very own voice –
        begging –
          demanding:
"Vladimir!
     Wait!
        Don't leave me!
Why didn't you just let me jump in the river then?
Run at those pillars and break my heart on them?"
Seven years standing here.
          Staring at that water
bound to those railings by ropes of verse.
Seven years the waves don't take their eyes off me.

Я уши лаплю.
    Напрасные мнешь!
Я слышу
       мой
          мой собственный голос.
Мне лапы дырявит голоса нож.

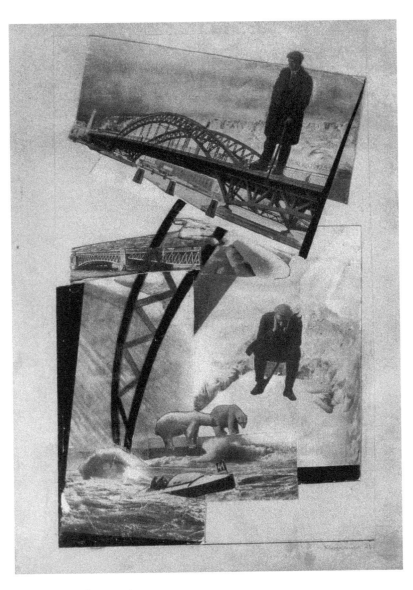

I paw at my ears
                kneading uselessly.
I hear
      my own
             my very own voice.
The knife of this voice bores through my paws.

Когда ж

    когда ж избавления срок?

Ты, может, к ихней примазался касте?

Целуешь?

   Ешь?

     Отпускаешь брюшко?

Сам

    в ихний быт

     в их семейное счастье

намереваешься пролезть петушком?!

Не думай!

   Рука наклоняется вниз его.

Грозится

   сухой

    в подмостную кручу. –

Не думай бежать!

   Это я

    – вызвал.

Найду

  Загоню

    Доканаю

      Замучу!

Там

   в городе

    праздник.

      Я слышу гром его.

Так что ж

   скажи чтоб явились они.

Постановленье неси – исполкомово.

Муку мою – конфискуй

         отмени.

Пока

   по этой

When, I ask,
           when will my sentence be up?
Are you sort of flogging
                  a dead horse?
Can you still kiss?
             Eat?
                  Grow a paunch?
You,
      with your fixation
                 on entering their lives,
their family happiness,
                 like an escaped cock!
"Don't even think of it!"
                  His hand gestures down
bone-dry
          into the gulf under the bridge.
"And don't think of running for it!
                      It was me
Who called you out."
He reiterated
"I'll find you
          Hunt you down
                Finish you off
                    Fix you!"
There
    in the city
        the holiday's begun.
                I can hear its noise.
Well OK.
      Tell them just to show up.
Hand them this resolution
            (from the Executive Committee).
Impound my torment.
              Call it off.
Just until

по Невской
по глуби
спаситель любовь
не придет ко мне
скитайся ж и ты
и тебя не полюбят.
Греби!
Тони меж домовых камней!

Спасите! Стой подушка!
Напрасное тщенье.
Лапой гребу –
плохое весло.
Мост сжимается.
Невским течением
меня несло
несло и несло.
Уже я далеко
Я может быть за день.
За день
от тени моей с моста.
Но гром его голоса гонится сзади.
В погоне угроз паруса распластал.
Забыть задумал невский блеск?!
Не заменишь?!
Не кем!
По гроб запомни переплеск
плескавший в „Человеке".
Начал кричать.
Разве это осилите?!
Буря басит

along Nevsky Prospect's[11]
                              far reaches
Love the saviour
                  comes to me
So you too
            can wander
                        unloved.
Row your boat!
            Drown among the city's stone blocks!
Save me!   Stop, ice pillow!
                              Your efforts are vain.
I row with my paw –
                        not much of an oar.
The bridge is shrinking.
                        The Neva's flow
Just carried me on
                  and on and on.
I'm already far away
                        A day's travel maybe.
A day's travel
            from my shadow on the bridge.
But still his voice comes thundering at my back.
My sail flattened by his threats
                              and exhortations.
Have you decided to forget
                        the gleam of the Neva?
Will you hand her over?!
                        Not for the world!
Death's oblivion
                  will still those splashing waves
Splashing still
            from our still sad *Humanity*.
I started to shout.
                  Is it too much for me?!
The gale rumbles

не осилить во век
Спасите! Спасите! Спасите! Спасите!
Там
на мосту
   на Неве
      человек!

II. НОЧЬ ПОД РОЖДЕСТВО.

Фантасти- Бегут берега
ческая   за видом вид.
реальность. Подо мной
         – подушка лед.
Ветром ладожским гребень завит.
Летит
      льдышка плот.
Спасите! – сигналю ракетой слов.
Падаю качкой добитый.
Речка кончилась –
      море росло
Океан
      – большой до обиды.
Спасите!
   Спасите!
         Сто раз подряд
реву батареей пушечной.
Внизу
      подо мной
            растет квадрат
остров растет подушечный.
Замирает – замирает
      замирает гул.
Глуше, глуше, глуше…

I can never defeat it.
Help! Help! Help! Help!
There, on the bridge
                    on the Neva,
                              there's a man!

II. CHRISTMAS EVE.

Magical
realism.

The shores race by
                    one prospect follows another.
Under me
            my icy pillow.
The Ladoga wind curls the waves to crests.
My raft of icicles
                    flies.
Help! – I send up a flare
                        of words.
And fall, done in by the rocking waves.
No more river –
                the swell of the sea
The ocean
            – vast to distraction
Help!
    Help!
            A hundred times in a row
I roar like a battery of cannons.
Down there
            beneath me
                        a rectangle grows,
pillowing.
Fading, fading,
            fading the rumbling.
Muffled and more muffled…

67

Никаких морей.
          Я
          — на снегу.
Кругом
          — версты суши.
Суша — слово.
          Снегами мокра.
Подкинут метельной банде я.
Что за земля?
          какой это край?
Грен
    лан
          люб-ландпя?

Боль были. Из облака вызрела лунная дынка
стену постепенно в тени оттеня.
Парк Петровский
    Бегу
          Ходынка
за мной.
          Впереди Тверской простыня.
А у у у!
          К Садовой аж выкинул „у!"
Оглоблей
    или машиной
но только
    мордой
          аршин в снегу.

What was that about sea?

                               I'm

                                      on the snow.

And all around

                  stretch arid miles of land.

Dry as language

                  but moistened by the snow.

I am given over

                  to the storm's bandits

What land is this?

                    Is this my native land?

Green-

     Lap-

        Love-land?

Kiss it better.   Ripens

            from out the cloud

                      a moony mist

Shadowing

          the wall

                with slow

                      shade.

The Petrovsky Park[12]

                I run

                  with Khodinka St.[13]

at my back,

           the sheet of Tverskaya[14]

                    ahead.

I howl like a mushroomer

                  combing the woods

crying to his friends "Coo-eeeeee!"

                    on the Ring Road.[15]

Felled by a carriage shaft

                  or squashed by a car

I lie flat

          stretched face down

                  in the snow.

Пулей слова матершины.
От нэпа ослеп?!
Для чего глаза впряжены?!
Эй ты!
    Мать твою разнэп!
Ряженый! –
Ох!
Да ведь
я медведь.
Недоразуменье!
    Надо
        прохожим
что я не медведь
    только вышел похожим.

Спаситель. Вон
    от заставы
        идет человечик.
За шагом шаг вырастает короткий.
Луна –
    голову вправила в венчик
Я уговорю
    чтоб сейчас же
        чтоб в лодке.
Это спаситель!
    Вид Иисуса
спокойный и добрый
    венчаный в луне.
Он ближе –

Shot with a bullet
　　　　　　of foul
　　　　　　　　　language.
"The bugger's blinded
　　　　　By the New Economic Bollocksy!?
He's wearing
　　　　bloody blinkers!
Hey you!
　　　　NEP[16] your fucking mother,
You Christmas goat!"
Oy! but you see
　　　　　　it's just me
　　　　　　　　the bear.
What a mix-up!
　　　　But actually I have to say
　　　　　　　　to passers-by
I'm not really a bear, I just
　　　　　　ended up looking like one.

The saviour.　Over there
　　　　　through the toll-gate
　　　　　　　　a small figure goes
With short steps
　　　　one by one
　　　　　　　progressing.
The moonlight
　　　　crowns his head
　　　　　　with a halo.
Can I persuade him
　　　　to fish my soul
　　　　　　　right now?
My Saviour!
　　　The revealed Christ
gentle and good
　　　　crowned by the moonlight.
From closer to –

71

лицо молодое безусо.
Совсем не Псус
    Нежней
        Юней.
Он ближе стал
    он стал комсомольцем.
Без шапки и шубы
    Обметки и френч
То сложит руки
    будто молится.
То машет
    будто на митинге речь.
Вата снег –
    Мальчишка шел по вате
Вата в золоте –
    Чего уж пошловатей!?
Но такая грусть –
        что стой
        и грустью ранься!
Расплывайся в процыганеннном романсе:

Романс. Мальчик шел в закат глаза уставя.
Был закат непревзойдимо желт.
Даже снег желтел к Тверской заставе.
Ничего не видя мальчик шел.
Шел
вдруг
встал.
В шелк
рук
сталь
С час закат смотрел глаза уставя

                        a youthful cleanshaven face.
Not Christ at all
                  Softer
                            Younger.
He drew closer
                  I saw his Komsomol[17] uniform.
No cap or overcoat
                            Leggings and high collar
The way his hands are
                        you'd think he's praying.
Now he's waving
                  like at some public speaker.
Cotton-woolly snow –
                        walking on cotton wool
Gold-wrapped cotton-wool –
                              the vulgarity of it!?
But the pity of it –
                  you can only stop
                        and finger your wounds!
Melt in a tearjerking gypsy romance:

Romance. A lad walked into the sunset
                              with downcast eyes.
Off into the exaggeratedly
                              yellow
                                    sunset.
The snow too was yellow at Tver St. tollgate.
The lad walked on seeing nothing.
Walked
then
stopped.
There was steel
in the silk
of his hands.
An hour or so he watched the sunset
                              tiring his eyes

за мальчишкой легшую кайму.
Снег хрустя разламывал суставы.
Для чего?
   зачем?
        кому?
Был вором ветром мальчишка обыскан.
Попала ветру мальчишки записка.
Стал ветер Петровскому парку звонить:
Прощайте…
    Кончаю…
        Прошу не винить…
До чего ж –
на меня похож!

Ничего не Ужас.
поделаешь.   Но надо ж!
          Дернулся к луже!
Залитую курточку стягивать стал.
Ну что ж товарищ!
   Тому еще хуже –
Семь лет он вот в это же смотрит с моста.
Напялил еле
   – другого калибра.
Никак не намылишься –
   зубы стучат.
Щерстищу с лапищ и с мордищи выбрил
Гляделся в льдину…
   бритвой луча…
Почти
   почти такой же самый.
Бегу

leaving a ribbon of footsteps

                          trailing behind him.

The crackling snow

                 strained all his joints.

What for?

       why?

             for someone?

The boy was strip-searched by the robber-wind.

A note he wrote fell into the wind's hands.

The wind sang out

                to Petrov Park:

Farewell…

       I'm putting an end…

                 Please don't blame me…

There's nothing you can do. What on earth –

he's just like me!

How horrible.

           Must it be like this!?

               Stumbling into a puddle

he started pulling off his sodden jacket.

Comrade! What the hell is all this?

              There are worse things –

Like seven years on my bridge

               watching: that's what.

I pulled it on with difficulty –

             it's the wrong size.

Can't lubricate it with a bit of soap –

              your teeth chatter.

I shaved my paws and muzzle clean

with a piece of ice for a mirror…

     and a moonbeam for a razor…

And I look

          almost exactly

Like myself.

I run

75

мозги шевелят адресами.
Во первых
　　на Пресню
　　　　туда
　　　　　　по задворкам –
Тянет инстинктом семейная норка.
За мной
　　всероссийские
　　　　теряясь точкой
сын за сыном
　　дочка за дочкой.
Володя!
　На Рождество!
Вот радость!
　　Радость-то во…
Прихожая тьма.
　　Электричество комната.
Сразу –
　　Наискось лица родни.

Всехные родители. Володя!
　　Господи!
　　　Что это?
　　　　В чем это? –
Ты в красном весь.
　　Покажи воротник!
Не важно мама
　　дома вымою.
Теперь у меня раздолье –
　　　　вода.
Не в этом дело.
　　Родные

with my brain boiling with addresses.
First of all
            to the Presnya[18]
                        beyond
                                    the backyards
– the family burrow drags me back by instinct.
At my back
the full complement of
relatives
            all Russia's
                        sons and daughters
dwindling to a dot
                        follow me.
Volodya!
            Here for Christmas!
What bliss!
            How happy you've made us all!
The lobby
            's in darkness!
The living room
                        's all electric,
Suddenly –
            Light's all over the faces of the relatives.

The full
complement
of relatives.

Volodya!
            Heavens!
                        What's this?
                                    What's going on?
You're all over red!
                        Show us your collar!
Never mind, mother
                        I can wash it at home…
I just have this feeling of expanding:
                                    Oceanic!
But that's not what…
                        – My nearest!

77

Любимые
Ведь вы меня любите?
любите?
Да?
Так слушайте ж!
Тетя!
Сестры!
Мама!
Тушите елку!
заприте дом!
Я вас поведу
вы пойдете
мы прямо
сейчас же
все
возьмем и пойдем.
Не бойтесь —
это совсем не далеко
600 с небольшим этих крохотных верст.
Мы будем там во мгновение ока.
Он ждет
Мы вылезем прямо на мост.
Володя
родной
успокойся! —
Но я им
на этот семейственный писк голосков:
Так что ж?!
Любовь заменяете чаем?
Любовь заменяете штопкой носков?
Не вы —

                              My dearest!
Do you really love me?
                    you love me?
                              Do you?
Well listen then!
                    Auntie!
                    My sisters!
                              Mother!
Put out the Xmas tree lights!
                              Lock the door!
I'll take you with me
                    you'll come too
                              straight there
right away
          we'll just grab everything
                              and go.
Don't be afraid –
                    it's no distance at all
Just 600 or so
          teeny little
                    vyorsts.[19]
We'll be there in the twinkling of an eye.
He's waiting
          we can just climb straight up that bridge.
Volodya!
          Darling!
                    Calm down!
                              But I howl
confronted by this
                    domestic
                              squeal:
WHAT?
          TEA INSTEAD OF LOVE??
You want to darn my socks INSTEAD?
It's not you –

                    79

Путешествие с мамой.

Не мама Альсандра Альсеевна
Вселенная вся семьею засеяна.
Смотрите
      мачт корабельных щетина –
в Германию врезался Одера клин.
Слезайте, мама,
      уже мы в Штеттине.
Сейчас,
   мама,
       несемся в Берлин.
Сейчас летите мотором урча вы:
Париж
     Америка
       Бруклинский мост
Сахара –
    и здесь
      с негритоской курчавой
лакает семейкой чаи негритос.
  Сомнете периной
        и волю
          и камень.
Коммуна
    и то завернется комом.
Столетия
    жили своими домками
и нынче зажили своим домкомом!

An excursion
with Mother.
It's that Alexandra Alexeyevna
The Mother in the poster
Of The Sower
Of Family Seeds.
Just look
a light growth
of ships' masts –
the Oder
has driven its wedge
into Germany.
Climb down, Mother,
we're in Stettin already.
And now,
Mother dear,
we'll move to Berlin.
Fly now
onwards
with your motor
rumbling
Paris
America
Brooklyn Bridge
the Sahara –
and here
with a curly-headed negress
a whole negro family laps up its tea.
A feather quilt turns your will to stone.
Even
The Family of Nations idea
turns homogeneous.
It's just centuries
of settlers
building their houses
followed by
residents' committees

Октябрь прогремел
            карающий
                судный
Вы
      под его огненерым крылом
расставились
      разложили посуды.
Паучьих волос не расчешешь колом.
Исчезни дом
      родимое место!
Прощайте!
      Отбросил ступеней последок.
Какое тому поможет семейство?!
Любовь цыплячья!
      Любвишка наседок!
Пресненсние Бегу и вижу
миражи.   всем в виду
Кудринскими вышками
себе навстречу
        сам
           иду
с подарками подмышками.
Мачт крестами на буре распластан
корабль кидает балласт за балластом.
Будь проклята

                              to tell us the rules.
When October thundered,
                    punishing,
                              judging,
You too
          under the firebird's wing
                              of Revolution
took your rightful places,
                    pushed aside the washing-up.
You can't
          brush away the cobwebs
                              with a stick.
Vanish!
          My parents' house
                              my dear native place!
Farewell!
          Shaking off the last dust
                              of the doormat.
What use is my family to me now?
With its scrawny old
                    chicken-shit love
its broody old hen
                    of lovey-dovey love!

Mirages of   I run and I see
the Presnya.   all laid out before me
The Kudrinsky watchtowers
                              coming towards me
I go to meet
          myself
                    with presents under my arm.
A ship flattened by the storm
                              its masts like crosses
A ship jettisoning ballast after ballast.
Damn this
          emptiness

83

опустошенная легкость! –
Домами оскалила скалы далекость.
Ни люда ни заставы нет.
Горят снега
              и голо
и только из-за ставенек
в огне иголки елок.
Ногам вперекор
              тормозами на быстрые
вставали стены окнами выстроясь.
По стеклам
              тени
                    фигурками тира
вертелись в окне
      зазывали в квартиры.
С Невы не сводит глаз
                          продрог
стоит и ждет –
                    помогут.
За первый встречный за порог
закидываю ногу.
В передней пьяный проветривал бредни.
Стрезвел и дернул стремглав из передней.
Зал заливался минуты две:
Медведь
      медведь

                                    weightlessness!
Distance
        discloses cliffs
                        – houses like snarling teeth.
No people no toll-booths.
Snow burns
                stripped bare
Christmas tree
                    needles feed
                                shuttered fires.
Feet drag
            braking their speed
walls line up
            their windows ranked like warriors.
On the glass
                shadows
                            figures on a rifle-range
spin on the glass
                    beckoning
                                to the flats.
Chilled to the marrow
                        his eyes glued
                                    to the Neva
he stands and waits –
                        Will help come?
I drag my foot over
                    the first doorstep.
In the entrance a drunk drying his fishing-nets.
Sobers up and darts headlong from the entrance.
The hall
            bursts into
                        two minutes' laughter:
Bear!
        Bear – oh!

медведь
медвееее!

Муж Феклы Давидовны со мной и со всеми знакомыми. Потом
    извертясь вопросительным знаком
хозяин полглаза просунул
   – однако!
Маяковский!
   Хорош медведь! –
Пошел хозяин любезностями медоветь:
Пожалуйста
   Прошу-с
      Ничего
       – я боком.
Нечаянная радость-с, как сказано у Блока.
Жена – Фёкла Двидна
Дочка
точь в точь
   в меня видно –
семнадцать с половиной годочков.
А это:…
   Вы кажется знакомы?! –
Со страха к мышам ушедшие в норы,
из-под кровати полезли партнеры.
Усища –
   – к стеклам ламповым пыльники –
из под столов пошли собутыльники.
Ползут с-под шкафа чтецы почитатели.
Весь безлицый парад подсчитать ли.
Идут и идут процессией мирной.

Bear – eee!

Bearchik!!

Then turning

with the quick sideways flick

of a question mark

the landlord stuck

his head out: Well I never!

Mayakovsky!

What a good bear you are! –

The landlord's

honeyed talk

flowed civilly on:

"Please!

I beg you

Don't mention it

Don't mind me!

An accidental happiness, sir

as Blok[20] puts it

My wife, a simple soul – Fyokia

My daughter

looks exactly like me –

just seventeen and a half

And then…

Do you two know each other?"

Escaping into any mouse-hole from fear

a couple climbed out from under the bed.

Big whiskers –

– round the shades on the lamp-glass –

A pair of drunks emerged from under the table.

Trying hard to understand

they creep

from under the cupboard.

How can we reckon

the whole faceless procession?

They all go their way, a harmless troupe.

87

Блестят из бород паутиной квартирной.
И это и стоит столетья
    как было.
Не бьют
    и не тронулась быта кобыла.
Лишь вместо хранителей духов и фей
ангел хранитель:
    жилец в галифе.
Но самое страшное:
    по росту
        по коже
одеждой
    сама походка моя! –
в одном
    узнал
        – близнецами похожи –
себя самого –
    сам
                я.
С матрацев,
    вздымая постельные трянки,
клопы, приветствуя, подняли лапки.
Весь самовар рассиялся в лучики –
хочет обнять в самоварные ручки.

They shine forth from the flat's
                    spidery beards.
So it ever was
            And ever shall be
                        World without end.
The old mare
            of the daily grind
                        canters on serenely.
Only instead of the familiar *lares* and *penates*
There's a red guardian angel:[21]
                    a lodger with trousers
                            tucked in his boots.
But the worst of it is
                    his stature
                            his skin
his clothes
            his gait
                    are mine! –
all in one go
            I recognised
                        – like two peas in a pod –
My
    Self –
            The Very
                    Me.
Raising
        from matresses
                        their tawdry bed-linen,
bedbugs
        waved their paws
                        in greeting.
The samovar[22]
                catching the light
                            shone all over
longing to enfold me

И это стоит столетья
          как было.
Не бьют
          и не тронулась быта кобыла.

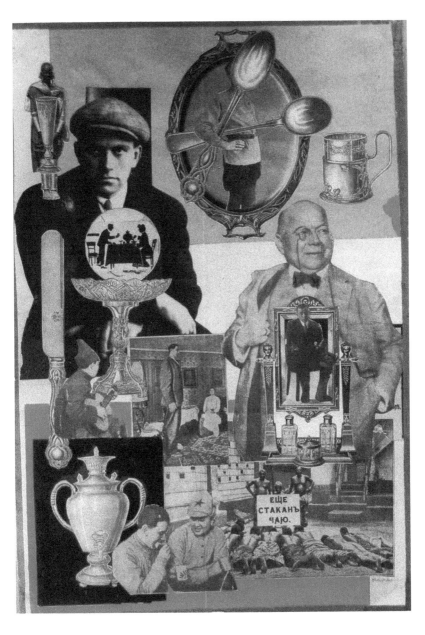

So it ever was
          And ever shall be
                    World without end.

91

В точках от мух
        веночки
            с обоев
венчают голову сами собою.
Взыграли туш ангелочки-горнисты,
проровев из иконного глянца.
Иисус,
        приподняв
            венок тернистый,
любезно кланяется.
Маркс,
        впряженный в алую рамку
и то тащил обывательства лямку.
Запели птицы на каждой на жердочке,
герани в ноздри лезут из кадочек.
Как были
        сидя сняты
            на корточках,
радушно бабушки лезут из карточек.
Раскланялись все
        осклабились враз;
кто басом фразу,
кто в дискант
        дьячком:
С праздничком!
    С праздничком!
        С праздничком!
            С праздничком!
С праз –
    нич –
        ком!
Хозяин

in its samovary arms.
Fly-spotted wreaths
made of wall-paper
crown the head
of yours truly.
Little cherubs playing horns
sounded a fanfare,
pink burns bright
in the icon's gleam.
Jesus, raising
his thorn-crown hat,
Bows politely.
And even Marx
harnessed in his scarlet frame
tugged on
the reins of routine.
Birds sing
from every perch.
Geraniums slither
up your nostrils
from flowerpots.
Genial grannies crawl
from photo-albums.
Everybody bows at once
and says "cheese";
one drones a bass
another a clerkly descant:
Merry Xmas!
Merry Xmas!
Merry Xmas!
Merry Xmas!
Merrrry
XXXX
CXertificate!
The landlord

то тронет стул,
        то дунет;
сам со скатерти крошки вымел:
Да я не знал!...
        Да я б накануне...
Да, думаю, занят...
        Дом...
                со своими...

Бессмысленные просьбы. Мои свои?
        Д-а-а-а –
                это особы.
Их ведьма, разве, сыщет на венике!
Мои свои
        с Енисея
                да с Оби
идут сейчас
        следят четвереньки.
Какой мой дом?!
Сейчас с него –
подушкой-льдом
плыл Невой –
мой дом
меж дамб
стал льдом
и там...
Я брал слова
        то самые вкрадчивые,
то страшно рыча
        то вызвоня лирово.
От выгод –
        на вечную славу сворачивал
молил,
        грозил,
                просил,

re-arrangXes

       the furnitXure

            puffXing;

and personally sweeps the crumbs

            from the table:

I had no idea!

      Yesterday I should have…

The house…

     Of course…

        Claims its Own.

Pointless   My kith and kin?

requests.   Yesssssss –

          they're special.

Like witches, perhaps, they fly on broomsticks!

My Siberian kith and kin

       from the Yenisei[23] and the Ob'

off they go

     or they track us down on all fours…

HOW IS THIS MY HOUSE?!

I just quit it –

on an ice-pillow, I

sailed the Neva –

my house is

between the flood-barriers

it turned to ice

and then…

I chose my words

      the most insinuating,

then roaring most horribly

     then plangent as a lyre.

Instead of just putting my case –

      I tried the eternal verities

I prayed,

   threatened,

      begged,

агитировал.
Ведь это для всех…
　　для самих…
　　　　для вас же…
Ну, скажем. Мистерия
　　– ведь не для себя ж?…
Поэт там и прочее…
　　ведь каждому важен…
Не только себе-ж
　　– ведь не личная блажь…
Я, скажем, медведь, выражаясь грубо…
Но можно стихи…
　　Ведь сдирают шкуру?!
Подкладку из рифм поставишь
　　　　– и шуба!…
Потом у камина…
　　там кофе…
　　　　курят…
Дело пустяшно:
　　ну, минут на десять…
Но нужно сейчас,
　　пока не поздно…
Похлопать может…
　　Сказать
　　　– надейся!…
Но чтоб теперь же…
　　чтоб это серьезно…
Слушали, улыбаясь, именитого скомороха.
Катали по столу хлебные мякиши.
Слова об лоб

turned bolshy.
– This is for everyone, see? For all…

It's all for YOU…
Can't you see? A sort of Mystery Play

– it's not for ME!
A poet, you see, and all that stuff

is ANYBODY'S
It's not just an ego-strip

some wanky sort of pose…
O.K. so I'm a bear, I talk pretty crude…
Poetry sort of…

Sort of strips off the skin!?
You fit a lining made of rhymes, and –

hey presto! A fur coat!…
They sit smoking…

drinking coffee…

by the stove
– It's such a trifling thing

takes just ten minutes…
But it has to be

NOW

before it's too late…
You can clap if you like…

and say

Dream on!…
But let it be NOW…

and the REAL THING…
They all listened

with a smile

to the famous clown.
Crumbs rolled

all over

the table.
Words struck

people's foreheads

97

и в тарелку
        горохом.
Один расчувствовался,
        вином размягший:
Поооостой…
        поооостой…
Очень даже и просто –
Я пойду!…
        Говорят, он ждет…
                на мосту…
Я знаю…
        Это на углу Кузнецкого моста.
Пустите!
        нукося!
По углам
        – зуд:
наззз-ю-зззюкался!
Будет ныть!   .
Поесть попить
попить поесть
и за 66!
Теорию к лешему!
Нэп
        – практика
Налей
        нарежь ему
Футурист –
        налягте-ка!
Ничуть не смущаясь челюстей целостью
пошли греметь о челюсть челюстью.
Шли
        из артезианских прорв
меж рюмкой

and plates
like peas.
One old wino was getting
tired and emotional…
Stooooop…
Shtopppppp…
Well a nod's as good as a wink –
I'll bugger off.
They say he's still waiting
on the bridge…
I know…
right by the corner of Kuznetsky Most.[24]
Out of my way!
Let me through!
A buzz like mosquitoes
fills the room
– He'sshh drrrunkk!
Cut out the whining!
– Let's eat! Let's drink!
– Let's drink! Let's eat!
– Let's have a game of cards!
Cheap at half the price
Marx can screw his theories
The New Economic Bollocksy
gets results.
Pour him vodka
Cut off his sausage
Bloody Futurist[25]
Squash the bugger.
Unabashed, mouths agape
chomping jaw against jaw,
the debate continued,
drawing from
Artesian torrents,
filling the glass

слова поэтических споров.
В матрац
                поздоровавшись
                                влезли клопы.
На вещи насела столетняя пыль.
А тот стоит –
                в перила вбит.
Он ждет,
                он верит:
                                скоро!
Я снова лбом
                я снова в быт
вбиваюсь слов напором.
Опять
                атакую и вкривь, и вкось.
Но странно:
                слова проходят насквозь.

Необычайное. Стихает бас в комариные трельки
Подбитые воздухом стихли тарелки
Обои
                стены
                                блекли…
                                        блекли…
тонули в серых тонах офортовых.
Со стенки
                на город разросшийся
                                        Беклин
Москвой расставил остров мертвых.
Давным давно.
                Недавно
теперь.

                              of poetic licentiousness.
Bedbugs
     exchanged greetings
                  as they crawled into the mattress.
The dust of centuries settled once more.
And there he stands
                        welded to his railings,
waiting,
        believing
                    that soon…
Headfirst
          into life's dreariness
                              I thrust again
With floods of words
                    on the attack
                            this way, that way…
But it's funny:
          my words just slip through
                    without touching the sides.
Most unusual. The bass voice subsides
                              in the mosquito choir
Plates stop rattling
                    as the fug gets to them
Wallpaper
          bleaches out…
                        bleaches out…
Drowned in grey-and-white
                        like an etching.
Böcklin's island
                grown
                        to the giant proportions
of the city of Moscow, leaves the wall
and heaps up its dead.
This happened long since.
But now

И нету проще!
Вон
   в лодке
      скутан саваном
недвижимый перевощик.
Не то моря
   не то поля –
их шорох тишью стерт весь.
А за морями
   – тополя
возносят в небо мертвость.
Чтож
   – ступлю!
   И сразу
     тополи
сорвались с мест
   пошли
      затопали.
Тополи стали спокойствия мерами,
ночей сторожами,
   милиционерами.
Расчетверившись
   белый Харон
стал коллонадой почтамтских коллон.

Деваться некуда.

Так с топором влезают в сон –
обмерят спящелобых
и сразу
   исчезает все
и видишь только обух.
Так барабаны улиц
       в сон
войдут

            of course
                        it's that much worse.
There you have him
                        in his boat
                                    bound in a shroud
The motionless ferryman.
Are those seas? Are they fields?
Their murmur
                is effaced quite.
And beyond the seas
                        the poplar trees
elevate death
            heavenwards.
So why not
            join them.
                        At once
                                    the trees
tear up their roots,
                        tread in black boots.
The poplars at intervals measure the silence
like security guards or policemen by night.
And pale Charon
                splits four ways
like the pillars
                on the Post Office portico.
Absolutely Choppers at the ready, in a dream
no way out.   climbing –
They take note of
                        the dreaming sleepers
and at once
                it all vanishes
and you see only
                        the wooden axe-butts.
So the drumming of the streets
                                    enters your dream

103

и сразу вспомнится —
что вот тоска
            и угол вон
за ним
        она
                    виновница. —
Прикрывши окна ладонью угла
стекло за стеклом вытягивал с краю
Вся жизнь
            на карты окон легла —
Очко стекла
            и я проиграю.
Арап —
        миражей шулер —
                        по окнам
разметил нагло веселия кран.
Колода стекла
            торжеством яркоогним
сияет нагло у ночи из лап.
Как было раньше —
                вырости-б
стихом в окно влететь.
Нет
        никни к стенной сырости.
И стих
        и дни не те.

and at once you come back to yourself.
You know it's just your depression.
Over there is the corner
and round the corner,
                    the girl
                            who is
to blame.
Covering the corners of the windows
                            with my palm
starting from the corner, I extracted
one pane after another
                    from its surround
like a pack of cards
                    you bet your life on.
What's my score in window-panes? am I
going to lose?
A little black guy,
                a neat sort of card-sharp,
has marked
            the panes
                    shamelessly.
What a joke! You crap-artist
A fist-full of glass
                    glittering festively
dazzles the night all at once.
I remember how it was
                    before all this –
growing like a poem
                    flying through the window.
Cut it out.
            You see that damp stain on the wall?
Give in to it.
            Poems
                and everything
                    ain't what they used to be.

Морозят камни.

    Дрожь могил

и редко ходят венники.

Плевками,

    снявши башмаки,

вступаю на ступеньки.

Не молкнет в сердце боль никак,

кует к звену звено.

Вот так,

    убив,

      Раскольников

пришел звенеть в звонок.

Гостьё идет по лестнице,…

Ступеньки бросил

    – стенкою.

Стараюсь в стенку вилесниться,

и слышу –

    струны тенькают.

Быть может села

      вот так

        невзначай она.

Лишь для гостей,

    для широких масс.

А пальцы

    сами

      в пределе отчаянья

ведут бесшабашье над горем глумясь.

Друзья. А вороны гости?!

    Дверье крыло

раз сто по бокам корридора исхлопано.

Горлань горланья,

    оранья орло

ко мне доплеталось пьяное допьяна.

Paving-stones are frosty,
                         tombstones shiver.
Rarely rarely comest thou O wreath-bearer.
Coughing and spitting,
                    and taking off my bast shoes,
I climb the steps, my pain
                         abating not a jot
hammering
           one link
                    to the next
the way Raskolnikov[26]
                       when he'd killed her
came ringing on the bell.
Bloody visitors
              all over the stairs…
I throw my best foot forward
                          hugging the wall
I try my hardest to melt into its mildew
and I hear how strings
                      tinkle.
Maybe
      she's just
                 sitting there
to please her guests
for all those bloody people.
And her fingers
               racked by despair
move thoughtlessly, mocking grief.
Friends.   They're carrion crows, not guests!?
The door over in the corridor bangs
                                  like a wing.
Bawlers bawl,
             howlers howl
drunks dead drunk
                 weave their way

107

Полоса
Щели
Голоса
еле:
Аннушка
       – ну и румянушка
Пироги…
    Печка…
Шубу…
    Помогает…
        С плечика…
Сглушило слова уанстепным темпом
и снова слова сквозь темп уанстепа:
Что это вы так развеселились?
Разве?!
    Слились…
Опять полоса осветила фразу.
Слова непонятны –
    особенно сразу.
Слова так
    (не то чтоб со зла):
„Один тут сломал ногу
так вот веселимся чем бог послал
танцуем себе понемногу“.
Да,
    их голоса
                знакомые выкрики.
Застыл в узнаванье,
        расплющился,
фразы крою по выкриков выкройке.
Да –
    это они –
        они обо мне.

In a line
        towards me.
Through a crack
                you can just make out
"Annushka-Rumyanushka"
                the way drunks sing.
Pies this way…
                Stove over here…
She helps them off
                with their fur coats…
Her words are drowned
                by the one-step rhythm
then again when it stops
                she confronts her men:
"Hey! say! why are you so gay?"
                They merged into one.
Again the crack
        lit up one phrase.
Unintelligible words –
                just blurted out.
Just words
        (they meant no harm):
"A bloke out there
                just broke his leg
so we're making the most
                of what God brings.
Let's have a dance."
Their voices are
                the same old screech.
I froze dumb,
        flattened by the knowledge
(I cut out patterns from their shouted words)
that they
        are talking
                about me.

Шелест.

  Листают наверное ноты

„Ногу говорите?

  Вот смешно-то!"

И снова

  в тостах стаканы исчоканы

и сыплют стеклянные искры из щек они.

И снова

  пьяное:

   „Ну и интересно!

Так, говорите, пополам и треснул?

Должен огорчить вас, как ни грустно,

не треснул, говорят.

  а только хрустнул."

И снова

  хлопанье двери и карканье

и снова танцы полами исшарканные.

И снова

  стен раскаленные степи

под ухом звенят и вздыхают в тустепе.

Только-б не ты. Стою у стенки

 Я не я.

Пусть бредом жизнь смололась

Но только б, только б не ее

невыносимый голос.

A whispering.
            Maybe they're riffling through
some music.
            "His leg you said?
What a hoot!"
Again the clink
            of glasses.
                  A toast!
And the sparks flash
            from the glasses
                  at their lips.
And again
        the drunken noise:
                "Well blow me down!
You say he just
        sort of cracked in two?"
"You'll be shocked to hear this
            but I have to tell you
he didn't crack, they say,
          he shattered, like glass."
The door bangs again, a great crowing
and more dancing
        and shuffling over the floors.
And again
        the walls
        baked hot like the steppe[27]
echo
    and sigh
        in my ears, in the two-step.

But not you too. I stand at the partition wall
          I am really not myself.
Let life
    rave on
but leave her out of this.
Her voice is

111

И снова
    стен раскаленные степи
под ухом звенят и вздыхают в тустепе.

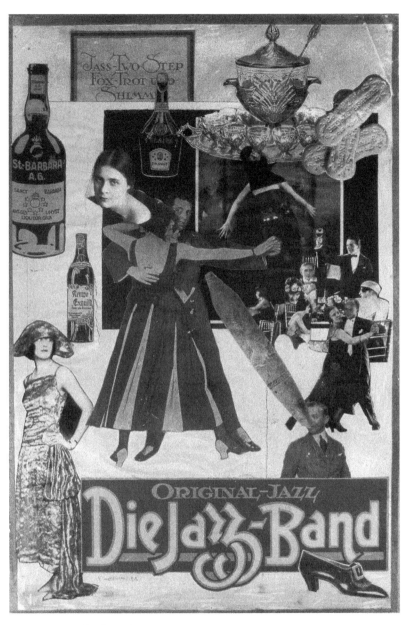

And again
       the walls baked hot like the steppe
echo and sigh in my ears, in the two-step.

Я день

    я год обыденщине предал

я сам задыхался от этого бреда.

Он

    жизнь дымком квартирошным выел.

Звал:

    решись

       с этажей

         в мостовые!

Я бегал от зова разинутых окон,

любя убегал –

    пускай однобоко

пусть лишь стихом

    лишь шагами ночными, –

Строчишь

    и становятся души строчными

и любишь стихом

    а в прозе немею,

Ну вот не могу сказать

    не умею. –

Но где, любимая,

    где, моя милая,

где

    – в песне!

        любви моей изменил я?

Здесь

    каждый звук

      чтоб признаться

       чтоб крикнуть.

А только из песни – ни слова не выкинуть

unbearable to listen to.
If I sacrificed a day
                    I sacrificed a year
To this dreary nonsense.
I too almost succumbed
                    to this delirium.
It ate up my life
                    with its domestic murk
and then said:
                    "Go on, jump
                                    from the first floor,
the pavement's waiting."
I ran from the summons
                    of gaping windows.
Loving, I ran away –
                    unrequited perhaps,
and maybe only in verse,
                    only with midnight steps,
Scribble, scribble
                    till souls turn to scribble
You love in verse
                    in prose turn dumb,
So I cannot say
                    I don't know how to.
But where, my darling,
                    where, my dearest,
where?
     – in a song!
                    Has my love changed, then?
Here
     every sound is
                    a confession
                                    a cry.
But from a song
                    you can't cut a single word.

Вбегу на трель
　　　　на гаммы.
В упор глазами
　　　　　　в цель!
Гордясь двумя ногами
Ни с места – крикну –
　　　　　　　　Цел!-
Скажу:
　　смотри
　　　　даже здесь, дорогая,
стихами громя обыденщины жуть
имя любимое оберегая
тебя
　　в проклятьях моих
　　　　　　　　обхожу.
Приди
　　разотзовись на стих
Я всех оббегав – тут.
Теперь лишь ты могла б спасти.
Вставай!
　　　Бежим к мосту!
Быком на бойне
　　　　　под удар
башку мою нагнул.
Сборю себя
　　пойду туда.
Секунда
　　и шагну.

Шагание стиха.

Последняя самая эта секунда
секунда эта
　　стала началом
началом

116

I run up into trills
                    into scales.
Staring fixedly
              at THAT!
Proud of my two legs
I'm not budging! INTACT! I cry.
Saying:
        just look
        even here, darling,
my poems demolish
                    the nightmare of dreariness
safeguarding the beloved name
I omit
      only You
              from my execrations.
Come
      give an answer
                    to my poems
I've done my share
              of Xmas visits.
Only you can help me now.
Up!
      Let us run to the bridge!
Like a bull to the slaughterhouse,
I bow
      my head
              to the blow.
Gather myself
            go where I must.
Just wait and see –
                  I'm off!
Verse Just at the last moment
marches that very moment
on.   there started up
        started up

117

невероятного гуда.
Весь север гудел.
  Гудения мало:
По дрожи воздушной
    по колебанью
догадываюсь
    – оно над Любанью.
По холоду
    по хлопанью дверью
догадываюсь
    оно над Тверью.
По шуму
    – настежь окна раскинул –
догадываюсь
    кинулся к Клину.
Теперь грозой Разумовское залил.
На Николаевском теперь
                    на вокзале.
Всего дыхание одно
а под ногой
        ступени
ношли
    поплыли ходуном
вздымаясь в невской пене.
Ужас дошел
    В мозгу уже весь
Натягивая нервов строй,
разгуживаясь все и разгуживаясь
взорвался
    пригвоздил:
        стой!
Я пришел из за семи лет

an incredible hooting.
The whole north
                hooted.
But the hooting wasn't the end of it:
judging by the shivering
                        and shaking
I conclude
        – it's over Luban.
Judging by the cold
                and the banging door
I guess
        – it's over Tver.[28]
From the noise
        – it banged the windows wide open –
I guess
        it's turned clean round towards Klin.
Now it fills
        Petrovskoye-Razumovskoye[29] station
with its din.
And now Nikolayevsky Station[30]
like a colossal breathing.
And underfoot
                the steps have gone
just floated away
                in all directions
rising on Neva's foam.
Horror descends.
                The brain is all stretched
the nerves frayed
                the hooting goes on and on
and I burst out
                pinning it all down:
                                Stop!
I have come

из за верст шести ста
пришел приказать:
      Нет!
Пришел повелеть:
 оставь!
Оставь.
  Не надо
    ни слова
      ни просьбы.
Чти толку?!
  Тебе
    одному
      удалось бы.
Жду
   чтоб землей обезлюбленной
           вместе
чтоб всей
  мировой
    человечьей гущей.
Семь лет стою –
  буду и двести
стоять пригвожденный
  этого ждущий.
У лет на мосту
   на презренье
    на смех
земной любви некупнтелем значась
дочжен стоять
  стою за всех –

                  seven years on
and from six hundred
                        vyorsts away
I have come
          in order to say:
                              No!
I have come
          to tell you:
                        Let it be!
Let it be.
        Stop it
              No words
                      No pleading.
What's the use?
                  Only you
                        could have
                              pulled it off.
I'll have to wait
                for love
                        to abandon the planet
when the loveless
                  multitudes
                        throng the earth.
Seven years I stand –
                    and will stand two hundred
nailed to this cross
                waiting, waiting.
On the bridge of the years
                        derided
                              laughed at
appointed
        the scapegoat
                    of earthly love
I must stand here
                standing in for

за всех расплачусь
            за всех расплачусь.
Ротонда.   Стены в тустепе ломались
                            на три
на четверть тона ломались
                    на сто…
Я, стариком,
        на каком-то Монмартре
лезу –
        – стотысячный случай –
        на стол.
Давно посетителям осточертело
Знают заранее
        все как по нотам:
Буду звать
        – (новое дело!)
куда-то итти
        спасать кого-то.
В извинение пьяной нагрузки
хозяин гостям объясняет:
                            русский!
Женщины
        мяса и трянок вязанки –
смеются
        стащить стараются

                                              everyone –
I have come to pay for all
                                              I will pay for all.
The Rotunda. The walls
                        split three ways
                                              in a two-step
          then split
                        into
                                 quarter-tones, and hundredths…
I, Tiresias,
                old man
                                 in some sort of Montmartre,
climb
          – for the hundred thousandth time –
                                              on a table.
The customers
                        were long since
                                              sick and tired
having learned the whole thing
                                              by heart.
I shall invite them
                        (for my next trick)
to go somewhere,
                        save someone.
Making excuses
                        for the poor old drunk,
the landlord
                        explains to the customers:
                                              A fine
specimen of Russian manhood!
The women,
                like meat
                                 swaddled in glad-rags,
just laugh –
                and try to pull me down

123

за ноги:
Не пойдем.
        Дудки.
Мы – проститутки.
Быть Сены полосе б Невой!
Грядущих лег брызгой
хожу по мгле по Сеновой –
всей нынчести изгой.
Саженный,
        обсмеянный
                саженный
                        битый
в бульварах
        ору через каски военщины:
Под красное знамя!
        Шагайте!
        По быту!
Сквозь мозг мужчины!
Сквозь сердце женщины!
Сегодня
        гнали
                в особенном раже.
Ну и жара же!
Полусмерть. Надо –
        немного обветрить лоб
Пойду
        пойду куда не вело б.
Внизу свистят сержанты трельщики

                                        by the feet.
"No way!
        Get stuffed!
We're on the game!."
Imagine if
        the Seine
                was a tributary of the Neva!
Spattered
        by the spray
                of the years to come
I walk
        in the dark
                on the Seine embankment
exiled from
        all of this present life of mine.
Keeping time
        (they laugh at me)
                keeping time
                        beating time
on the boulevards
        I howl over the military helmets:
"Red banner aloft!
                Best foot forward!
                        A better life for all!
Through the brains of men!
Through the hearts of women!"
Today
        they pressed forward
                in a great fury.
What passion.
Half dead.   I really must
                cool off a bit
I'll go
        wherever the wind blows.
Down below

125

Тело

    с панели

        уносят метельщики

Рассвет,

    подымаясь сенскою сенью,

    синематографской серой тенью.

Вот!

      Гимназистом смотрел их —

                      с парты —

мелькают сбоку Франции карты.

Воспоминаний последним током

тащился прощаться

      к странам Востока.

Случайная станция. С разлету рванулся —

    и стал

      и на мель

Лохмотья мои зацепились штанами

Ощупал —

    скользко —

      луковка точно.

Большое очень.

    Испозолочено.

Под луковкой

    колоколов завыванье.

Вечер зубцы стенные выкаймил.

126

                    traffic-cops whistle
Street-sweepers
                    lift a corpse
                              off the pavement.
Dawn.
I climb
        through the Seine's shadows,
a movie-land black-and-white.
Look!
        Like a schoolboy
                    at his desk
I watched them
                flash over
                        the map of France.
One last surge
            of memories
which dragged itself up,
        to say goodbye
                to me, the mysterious Orient.
Home quite   From these flights
by chance.   I fled
                        and stood
feeling firm ground underfoot.
I touched
        my rags
                held together
                            by my trousers.
Slimy, like
        the skin of an onion.
A gigantic
        gilded
            onion
                dome
filled with the howling of bells.
Evening fringed the walls' crenellations.

На Иване я
Великом.
          Вышки кремлевские пиками.
Московские окна
          видятся еле.
Весело
          Елками зарождествели.
В ущелья кремлевы волна ударяла
то песня
          то звона рождественский вал,
С семи холмов
          низвергаясь Дарьялом
бросала Тереком
                    праздник
                    Москва.
Вздымается волос.
          Лягушкою тужусь.
Воюсь –
          оступлюсь на одну только пядь
и этот
     старый
          рождественский ужас
меня
          по Мясницкой закружит опять.

Повторение пройденного. Руки крестом
          крестом
               на вершине,
ловлю равновесие,
          страшно машу.
Густеет ночь
          не вижу в аршине.
Луна.

And I sit
        on
                Ivan's church
                        feeling terrible.
The Kremlin towers are like spears.
You can just see Moscow's windows.
Cheery
        with their Christmas trees.
A wave broke
                over the Kremlin's caverns
now singing
        and now
                a Christmas billow of bells,
Moscow's holy day
    streams down
        from the Terek[31] and the Daryal[32]
over the seven hills.
My hair stands on end
                        I strain like a croaking frog
and I am afraid
                and I take just one step back
and this old
        Christmas
                terror
swarms round me
        – like on Myasnitskaya –
                        all over again.

Compulsive repetition. On the cathedral roof
                my arms
                        are cruciform,
I catch my balance
                waving frantically.
Night thickens
                can't see an inch.
The moon...

129

Ловлю равновесие,
страшно машу.

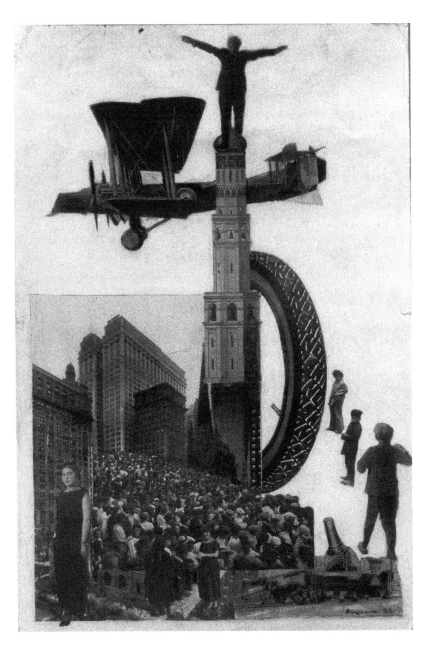

I catch my balance
          waving frantically.

Подо мною
      льдистый Машук.
Никак не справлюсь с моим равновесием
Как будто с Вербы –
      руками картонными
заметят
      Отсюда виден весь я.
Смотрите –
      Кавказ кишит Пинкертонами.
Заметили
      Всем сообщили сигналом.
Любимых
    друзей
      человечьи ленты
со всей вселенной сигналом согнало.
Спешат рассчитаться
      идут дуэлянты.
Щетинясь
   щерясь
      еще и еще там
плюют на ладони
    ладонями сочными,
руками,
   ветром,
     нещадно.
      без счета
в мочалку щеку истрепали пощечинами.
Пассажи –

While under me
Mashuk[33] gleams icily.
Nohow can I get my equipoise back
Like an osier
recognisable
by its papery hands
I am all too visible here.
Just look
the Caucasus
is crawling
with American agents.
They've spotted me
and passed the signal on
to everyone.
A human tape-worm
of their chums
infests the universe
roused by their signal.
They have old scores
they rush
to settle.
Duellers bristling
baring their teeth
So many
With ham fists
spitting in their palms
Arms flailing
a whirlwind
merciless
innumerable!
Slaps
round the kisser
with a wet
loofah!
Arcades-full

перчаточных лавок початки
дамы
        духи развевая паточные
снимали
        в лицо швыряли перчатки
швырялись в лицо магазины перчаточные.
Газеты,
        журналы,
            зря не глазейте!
На помощь летящим в морду вещам
ругней
        за газетиной взвейся газетина.
Слухом в ухо!
        Хватай клевеща!
И так я калека в любовном боленьи.
Для ваших оставьте помоев ушат.
Я вам не мешаю.
        К чему оскорбленья.
Я только стих
        я только душа.

of glove shops
                    stripped bare.
                              as a corn-cob.
Ladies
     in a waft
            of honey-sweet scent
stripped off
            their gloves
                    to fling in my face.
Whole shopfuls.
                    Don't even mention
                              all that
magazine
        and newspaper
                    gossip!
Just get stuck in,
            and bawl in the face
                              of events.
Let the scribblers
                scribble
                    their evil fill.
Pour rumour in his ears!
            Shove slander down his throat!
What am I but
            a cripple
                    infected
                        with love.
A sort of
        empty vessel
                you can fill
                          with your shit.
I will not stop you.
                    What use are these insults?
I'm just a poem
            I'm just a state of mind.

А снизу:
    Нет!
        ты враг наш столетний
Один уж такой попался –
    Гусар!
Понюхай порох,
        свинец пистолетный.
Рубаху в распашку!
        Не празднуй труса!

Последняя смерть.
Хлеще ливня,
      грома бодрей
бровь к брови
      ровненько
со всех внитовок
      со всех батарей
с каждого маузера н браунинга
с сотни шагов
    с десяти
      с двух
в упор –
      за зарядом заряд.
Станут чтоб перевесть дух
и снова свинцом сорят.
Конец ему!
    В сердце свинец!
Чтоб не было даже дрожи!
В конце концов
– всему конец.
Дрожи конец тоже.

То что осталось.
Окончилась бойня.
    Веселье клокочет.
Смакуя детали, разлезлись шажком.
Лишь на Кремле

And underneath all that
                    just the old enemy.
One of them's already copped it –
                        a gay hussar!
Get a niff of the gun-powder
                    the gun-metal.
Shirt wrenched open!
                    No quarter for cowards!
My last death. Overwhelming as a deluge,
                    deafening as thunder
eyeball
        to eyeball
                from every rifle
                        and field-gun
from every Mauser and Browning
at a hundred paces
                or ten
                    or two
point-blank –
                round after round.
They pause to draw breath
then splash out lead again.
That's got him!
                Lead straight to the heart!
Not so much as a shudder!
When all's said and done
                    – that's done him!
Done his bloody shudders in as well.
What's left   The knacker's
of me.   yard
                    is over.
Merrymaking gurgles.
Relishing the details
                    they sprawled
while in the Kremlin

поэтовы клочья
сняли по ветру красным флажком.
Да небо
	по прежнему
		лирикой звездится.
Глядит
	в удивленье небесная звездь:–
Затрубадурила Большая Медведица.
Зачем?
		В королевы поэтов пролезть?
Большая,
	неси ко векам Араратам
сквозь небо потопа
	ковчегом ковшом.
С борта
	звездолетом
		медведьинским братом
горланю стихи мирозданию в шум.
Скоро!
	Скоро!
		Скоро!
В пространство!
	Пристальней!
Солнце блестит горы.
Дни улыбаются с пристани.

        the poet's cast-offs
shone
    in the wind
        like the Red Flag.
And the sky
     just like before
          is starred with lyrics.
The heavenly
     shiners
       look on
         in wonder:
The Great Bear goes a-Minstrelling
What for?
     To creep up on
        The Queen of all the Poets?
O beary one,
      through the heaven of the flood
take the Plough as your ark
        after Ararat's[34] centuries!
On board
    the spacecraft
       the brother of a bear
shouts verses:
      some racket
        about the creation.
Quick!
   Quick!
     Quick!
Journey into space!
        Don't take your eyes off it!
The sun
    illumines
      the hill-tops.
The days
     smile in welcome
        from the landing-stage.

ПРОШЕНИЕ НА ИМЯ...
(Прошу вас, товарищ химик, заполните сами!)

Пристает ковчег.
   Сюда лучами!
Пристань.
   Эй!
Кидай канат ко мне!
И сейчас же
   ощутил плечами
тяжесть подоконничьих камней.
Солнце
   ночь потопа высушило жаром.
У окна
   в жару встречаю день я.
Только с глобуса – гора Калемаджаро
Только с карты африканской Кения.
Голой головою глобус.
Я
   над глобусом
     от горя горблюсь.
Мир
   хотел бы
     в этой груде горя
настоящие облапить груди горы.

APPLICATION ON BEHALF OF...
(Please, comrade chemist, fill it in yourself)

The Plough reaches the shore.
                    Lights, over here!
The landing-stage.
                    Hey!
Throw me a rope!
And at once
                I felt on my shoulders
the weight
            of great
                    window-sills.
The sun
        has dried
            the night's flood
                        with its heat.
By the window
            I greet
                    in heat
                        the day.
Straight from the globe
                    Mount Kilimanjaro
Straight from the atlas
                    the map of Kenya.
O globe with the bald head.
I hunch
        and munch
                my grief
                        on this globe.
Peace
    and the universe
                    's all my grieving
                                breast seeks.
Pawing
        the real
                breast
                    of grief.

Чтобы с полюсов
       по всем жильям
лаву раскатил горящ и каменист
так хотел бы разрыдаться я
медведь – коммунист.
Столбовой отец мой
                дворянин,
кожа на моих руках тонка.
Может
      я стихами выхлебаю дни
и не увидав токарного станка.
Но дыханием моим,
      сердцебиеньем,
             голосом,
каждым острием издыбленного в ужас волоса,
дырами ноздрей,
      гвоздями глаз,
зубом искрежещенным в звериный лязг,
ежью кожи
      гнева брови сборами,
триллионом пор
      дословно –
          – всеми порами

From the poles
   through all the arteries
rolling
 lava
  burning
   molten stone
sobbing. This is all
a communist bear
   has to hope for.
My old man
  was gentry,
I have thin skin on my hands.
Maybe
 verse
  just gobbles up my days –
I wouldn't recognise
 a turner's lathe
  if I woke up in bed with one.
But my breathing,
  my heartbeat,
   my voice,
and every hair
  standing on end
   in horror,
the holes
 of my nostrils,
the nails
 banged through my eyes
Teeth
 clashing together
   like fangs,
a hedgehog's spines
  eyebrows knitted in rage,
a trillion times over
  – seriously! –

в осень,
    в зиму,
       в весну,
          в лето
в день,
    в сон
не приемлю
    ненавижу это
все.
Все
    что в нас
       ушедшим рабьим вбито
Все
    что мелочинным роем
оседало
    и осело бытом
даже в нашем
    краснофлагом строе.
Я не доставлю радости
видеть
    что сам от заряда стих.
За мной не скоро потянете,
об упокой его душу таланте.
Меня
    из за угла
       ножом можно.
Дантесам в мой не целить лоб.
Четырежды состарюсь – четырежды

                                        any old time at all,
Autumn
        Winter
                Spring
                        Summer
day-time,
        dream-time,
I cannot accept it
I hate it
All of it.
Everything
        that chains us
                        to a past of slavery,
Everything
        the vulgar
                slave-swarm
alighted upon,
        everything
                routine
                        swarmed over
even in our
        red-bannered
                        order of things.
It gives me no pleasure
to see
        that I'm alone in the poets' brigade!
In time you'll be taking pot-shots at me
to keep your talent warm
or you'll fix me
        with a knife
                round some dark corner!
No noble assassin
        as in Pushkin's case
                        will take careful aim.
Four times I try –

Четырежды состарюсь – четырежды
омоложенный

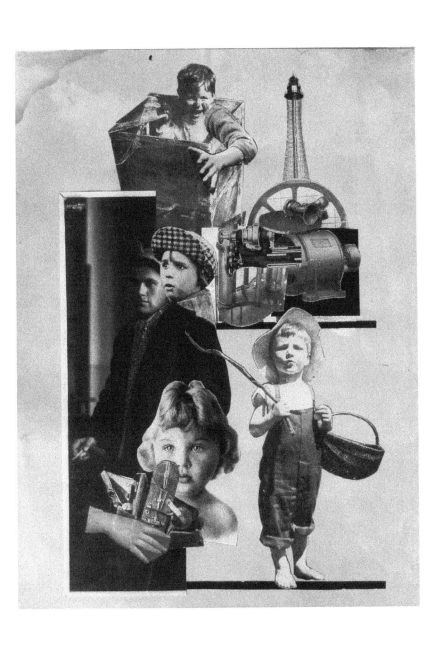

Four times I try – four times
a child again

омоложенный

до гроба добраться чтоб.
Где б ни умер
      умру – поя.
В какой трущобе ни лягу
знаю
      достоин лежать я
с легшими под красным флагом.
Но за что ни лечь –
      смерть есть смерть.
Страшно не любить –
      ужас – не сметь.
За всех – пуля
      за всех – нож.
А мне когда?
      А мне то чтож?
В детстве, может,
      на самом дне,
десять найду
      сносных дней.
А то что другим!
      Для меня б этого!
Этого нет.
      Видите –
        – нет его!
Верить бы в загробь!
      Легко прогулку пробную.
Стоит
      только руку протянуть –
пуля
      мигом
        в жизнь загробную
начертит гремящий путь.

                    four times
                              a child again
getting myself all ready for the tomb.
If I have to die
              I'll go down singing.
Whatever hole I lie in
I know I'm fit
to lie alongside the red standardbearers.
But lie where you will –
                          death is death.
How terrible
              not to love –
              horrible not to dare.
Just a bullet
              to end it all –
or a knife.
When is it my turn?
                          And what will it look like?
In childhood, maybe,
if I dig deep enough
I can find perhaps ten
bearable days.
They're what I want!
Let others have what they may.
– But no, you can't.
    Look –
          all gone!
To believe in the afterlife!
    Easy to make a dummy run.
Stand and
              just stretch out your hand.
One bullet
              zips you through
                              to the other side,
marks its passage with a roar.

Что мне делать
        если я
                во всю
всей сердечной мерою
в жизнь сию
сей
        мир
                верил,
                        верую.
Вера. Пусть во что хотите жданья удлинятся —
        вижу ясно
                ясно до галлюцинаций.
До того
        что кажется —
                вот только с этой рифмой
                                развяжись
и вбежишь
        по строчке
                в изумительную жизнь.
Мне ли спрашивать —
        да эта ли?
                Да та ли?!
Вижу
        вижу ясно до деталей.
Воздух в воздух
        будто камень и камень
недоступная для тленов и крошений
рассиявшись
        высится веками
мастерская человечьих воскрешений.
Вот он
        большелобый
                тихий химик
перед опытом наморщил лоб.

What am I to do
            if I
                  believed
                        and still believe
to the limit
            of my credulity
in this world
            – this one –
                        with all my heart?
Belief.   You can wait
                  as long as you like
                              for whatever –
but I see clearly
                  as if I was
                              hallucinating.
And it seems to me
                  if you can find the rhyme
a line can
            run on
                  to a new-created life.
If you ask me –
            Is it like this? Or like that?
I just see –
            see clearly and in detail –
air, air,
            or the stone. The stone.
No dust corrupts it. It does not decay.
It will shine out
                  towering through the ages,
workshop of human resurrection.
Regard him
            the quiet, highbrowed
                              chemist
before the experiment
                  his brow is furrowed

151

Книга –

   „вся земля”–

     выискивает имя.

Век XX-ый.

   Воскресить кого б?

– Маяковский вот...

   поищем ярче лица, –

недостаточно поэт красив.–

Крикну я

   вот с этой

     с нынешней страницы:

– не листай страницы!.

   Воскреси!

Надежда. Сердце мне вложи

   кровищу –

     – до последних жил.

В череп мысль вдолби!

Я свое, земное, не дожил

на земле

   свое не долюбил.

Был я сажень ростом.

   А на что мне сажень?

Для таких работ годна и тля.

Перышком скрипел я в комнатенку всажен.

вплющился очками в комнатный футляр.

Что хотите буду делать даром –

His book –
     "the entire planet"–
          he searches for a name.
Resurrect someone?
         In the twentieth century?
– Mayakovsky for example?…
     We could find someone better –
Just some pretty poet
        won't do.
I cry
   from off
      this very same
         page:
– Quit riffling!
      Resurrect me!

Hope. Give me blood,[35]
      Fill my heart,
         Every last vein,
Ram thoughts into my skull!
I'm not finished yet
      with earthly life,
Not finished
    with love
      on this planet.
I once was seven foot tall
      But what use is this seven foot?
A louse
   could do as much.
My plumage
    jabs and scrapes
       in my little room.
My eyes
    are squashed flat
       by this box of mine.
Just say the word, I'll do it all

153

чистить

    мыть

        стеречь

            мотаться

                месть.

Я могу служить у вас

    хотя б швейцаром.

Швейцары у вас есть?

Был я весел –

    толк веселым есть ли

Если горе паше непролазно,

нынче,

    обнажают зубы если

только чтоб хватить

    чтоб лязгнуть.

Мало ль что бывает –

    тяжесть

        или горе...

Позовите!

    пригодится шутка дурья.

Я шарадами гипербол

    аллегорий

буду развлекать

    стихами балагуря.

Я любил...

    Не стоит в старом рыться.

Больно?

    Пусть...

        Живешь и болью дорожась

Я зверье еще люблю –

    у вас

        зверинцы

            есть?

Пустите к зверю в сторожа.

                              for nowt –
cleaning
     washing
          care-taking
               lurking
                    fixing someone.
I could really be some use to you –
I'd make a good door-man.
Do you need a door-man by any chance?
I once used to be cheerful –
                    Need an expert on cheerfulness?
Got a case of grief? The real thing?
These days
          folks snarl
               if you just touch them
                    their teeth chatter.
Who knows what might turn up –
               misery
                    or grief…
Give me a call!
                    A daft joke may be just the thing.
I'm good at
          charades
               hyperboles
                    allegories
for passing the time, a comic turn.
I once used to love…
               No point in rummaging in the past.
Does it hurt?
     Maybe…
          Life keeps raising the pain stakes
I still like animals –
               Got any little furry animals?
If you want some animals protecting

Я люблю зверье —
      увидишь собаченку —
тут у булочной одна —
      сплошная плешь —
из себя
      и то готов достать печенку.
Мне не жалко дорогая
      — ешь!

Любовь. Может
      может быть
         когда-нибудь
           дорожкой зоологических
               аллей
и она
      — она зверей любила —
         тоже ступит в сад
улыбаясь
      вот такая
         как на карточке в столе.
Она красивая —
      ее наверно воскресят.
Ваш
      тридцатый век
         обгонит стаи
сердце раздиравших мелочей.
Нынче недолюбленное
      наверстаем
звсздностью бесчисленных ночей.
Воскреси
      хотя б за то
         что я
           поэтом
ждал тебя,

I really like animals –
        if you see a dog –
there's one here by the baker's shop –
        all over lashes –
straining
        to get at the cakes.
I grudge you
        nothing
            darling –
Eat!

Love.   Perhaps
    perhaps, just once,
        entering the path in the zoo section
she too
    – she used to like animals –
        will come to the Public Gardens,
smiling
    the way she looks
        in that photo on the table.
She's beautiful –
    I'm sure they'll resurrect her.
Your
    thirtieth century
        will leave all the rest far behind,
all the heart's harrowing trivia.
At that point in time
    we'll make up for
        all the aggravation
with the starriness
    of a thousand and one
        nights.
Resurrect then!
    If only because
        I am a poet
and I've been waiting for you,

и она
    — она зверей любила —
        тоже ступит в сад

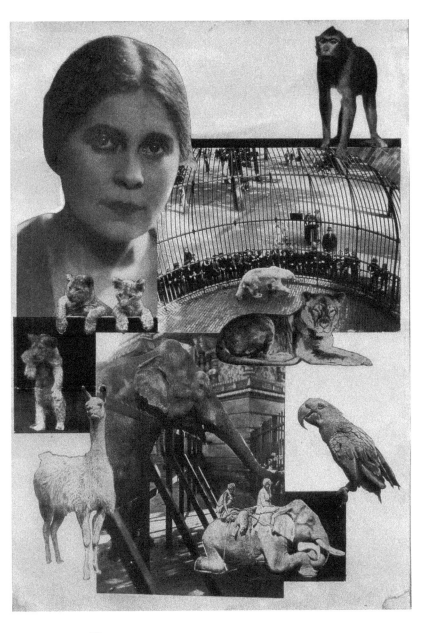

She too
    – she used to like animals –
        will come to the Public Gardens

откинул будничную чушь.
Воскреси меня
          хотя б за это!
Воскреси –
          свое дожить хочу!
Чтоб не было любви – служанки
замужеств
               похоти
                    хлебов
Постели прокляв,
          встав с лежанки
чтоб всей вселенной шла любовь
Чтоб день
          который горем старящ
не христарадничать, моля.
Чтоб вся
          на первый крик:
               – товарищ! –
оборачивалась земля.
Чтоб жить
          не в жертву дома дырам.
Чтоб мог
          в родне
               отныне
                    стать
отец –
          по крайней мере миром
землей по крайней мере – мать.

I've chucked out
          all the other old
                  rubbish.
Resurrect me just on that account!
Resurrect! I have so
          much living still to do.
Let there be no more love
          like a timid handmaiden.
Let there be no more marriages of
              lust-and-potatoes.
Curse beds,
      get up you supine fool.
Let love
      make its universal music.
Give us this day
          grown old with grief
a reprieve from Christ's
          sanctimoniousness.
Let the whole planet
        turn
          with one cry:
– Comrade! –
Not sacrificing our lives
      in domestic holes and corners.
The Universe be
      Our Father
          in Our Family
             from now on
And the Earth, come what may,
          Our Mother.

Translated by Larisa Gureyeva
and George Hyde

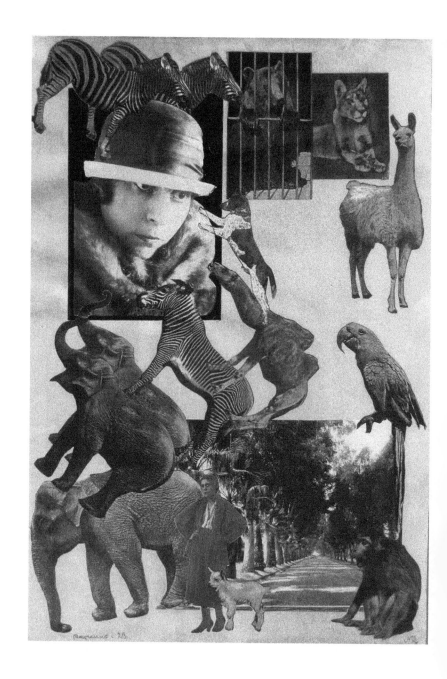

[Untitled]

162

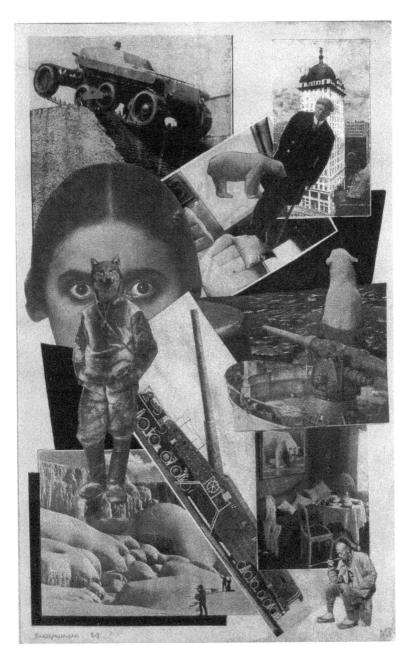

[Untitled]

NOTES

[1] *The Caucasus:* the highest range of mountains in the south of Russia, marking one of its boundaries. The Caucasus connotes danger, the exotic and the erotic and has furnished a rich literature in Russian as well as the national languages of the area.

[2] *The River Neva:* the river on which St. Petersburg (formerly Leningrad) was built to embody what Pushkin described as "a window on the West". Russian literature records the elemental danger of the river and the inhospitality of the nineteenth-century capital to its multitudes of rootless inhabitants.

[3] *Lubyansky Passage:* a small street in Moscow.

[4] *Vodopyany:* a small street in Moscow.

[5] *Myasnitskaya:* a large street in Moscow (the "ploughlands" reference is ironic).

[6] *Danthes:* the courtier who killed Aleksander Pushkin in a duel. This was ostensibly a love-conflict but may have been politically motivated. Pushkin was Russia's greatest poet, who forged the norms and forms of literary Russian for more than a century. Aleksandr Sergeyevich Pushkin has something in common with Byron but does not read well in English.

[7] *All-Union Executive Committee:* a special government department in the early days of the Soviet Union (1917-19), responsible for the "red terror" (summary execution of opponents of the Bolsheviks).

[8] *The Erfurt Programme:* the programme of the German Social-Democrat party, adopted in Erfurt in 1891 and influenced by Engels. Lenin admired it, but also criticised it for lacking the politically crucial idea of the "dictatorship of the proletariat".

[9] *Izvestiya*: along with *Pravda* (Truth), *Izvestiya* (News) was the most important daily paper in the USSR. Between them they reproduced Party ideology to such a degree that an old joke went around: "What is the difference between *Izvestiya* and *Pravda*?" (V *Izvestii* nyet pravdy, i v *Pravdie* nyet izvestii?) – "In the news there's no truth, and in the truth there's nothing new."

[10] *Lake Ladoga:* a lake in the north of Russia close to St. Petersburg and the site of many historic conflicts between Russia

164

and her Northern neighbours.

[11] *Nevsky Prospekt:* the main thoroughfare of St. Petersburg. Gogol's short story of this title is one of the seminal texts of nineteenth-century Russian literature. As a Ukrainian, Gogol was well equipped to express the sense of alienation that is the keynote of "the Petersburg theme".

[12] *Petrovsky Park:* a large park in Moscow which now houses the Dynamo Football Club. Dostoevsky's Raskolnikov alludes to it with distaste (cf. note 26).

[13] *Khodinka St.:* a street in Moscow.

[14] *Tverskaya St.:* formerly Gorky St. and (informally) Piterskaya, this is the most splendid of Moscow's great radial streets.

[15] *Ring Rd.:* in present-day Moscow, with its enormous increase in car ownership, the Ring Rd. is now much more crowded than in Mayakovsky's day and it's hard to imagine such a scene as he describes.

[16] *N.E.P.:* Lenin's New Economic Policy (1921) gave more freedom in the labour market to the peasantry, who were allowed to keep some of their surpluses. Private enterprise was reintroduced to make distribution and consumption easier, though there were still so few goods to buy that those who had money tended to keep it, causing inflation. The rationale of this radical departure from communist orthodoxy was to help to build up the capital needed to bring Soviet industry up to a global level. It didn't work. Mayakovsky joined the Old Guard in denouncing this new economic tendency, mainly on the grounds that it led at once to corruption and profiteering (cf. Bulgakov in *The Master and Margarita*).

[17] *Komsomol:* the abbreviation of the Russian for Communist Union of Youth, the youth wing of the Communist Party, founded in 1918 and active until very recently. People between the ages of 14 and 28 were eligible to join (under-14s were Pioneers). About two-thirds of present-day Russian citizens were once in the Komsomol. Members wore a special red banner badge with Lenin's profile.

[18] *Presnya:* a square and street close to the centre of Moscow.

[19] *vyorst:* an obsolete Russian measurement of length or distance, equal to 500 sazhen (3,500 feet).

[20] *Aleksander Blok:* Blok (1880-1922), was an important Symbolist poet whose metaphysical pursuit of the Unknown Woman, pronounced urbanism and fusion of apocalyptic Christianity with Marxist politics (in *The Twelve*) may all be said to have influenced Mayakovsky, despite their profound temperamental differences.

[21] *red guardian angel:* the Soviet Army was known as the Red Army between 1918 and 1941. The "angelic" connotation is probably indebted to Blok.

[22] *samovar:* a large Russian tea-kettle, traditionally fired by charcoal. The teapot sits on top to keep hot.

[23] *Yenisei:* with the Ob', one of the two longest rivers in Siberia.

[24] *Kuznetsky Most:* an old street in the centre of Moscow, close to Lubyanka Square and famous for its art-bookshops.

[25] *Futurism:* Mayakovsky was a founder-member of the Russian Futurists, representing the Cubist, radical wing of the movement which interacted with Constructivism, Suprematism and other abstract conceptual tendencies. The early Futurists were iconoclastic and Bohemian and these lingering tendencies in the new Socialist bard greatly perturbed the Communist authorities. They tried to obliterate them, just as they airbrushed Lily out of photographs of the couple.

[26] *Raskolnikov:* the hero of Dostoevsky's *Crime and Punishment* (cf. note 13).

[27] *Steppe:* vast areas of central Russia where nothing but grass grows, scorched by the extreme heat.

[28] *Tver:* formerly Kalinin, a city in northern Russia situated on the confluence of the Volga and the Tvertsa rivers.

[29] *Petrovskoye-Razumovskaya:* a small railway station in Moscow.

[30] *Nikolayevsky:* a railway station in St. Petersburg.

[31] *Terek:* a river in the Caucasus, featured in Tolstoy's *The Cossacks*.

[32] *Daryal:* a river in the Caucasus.

[33] *Mashuk:* a mountain in the vicinity of Piatigorsk, a resort town in the Caucasus featured in Lermontov's *A Hero of Our Time.*

[34] *Ararat:* the mountain in Armenia where Noah's Ark came to rest.

[35] *Blood transfusion:* the Belorussian scientist and author Mikhail Bogdanov (1873-1928) became very interested in blood transfusion after noting its rejuvenating effects in experiments on himself. As a consequence, he was entrusted with Lenin's brain and the eventual resuscitation of the Bolshevik leader. Mayakovsky's fascination with Christian eschatology and his incongruous material transpositions of it climax in this ironic assertion of his claims to "immortality", inspired by Bogdanov (who was also a talented writer of science fiction, but as one of the figureheads of Proletkult not much to Mayakovsky's liking).

BIOGRAPHICAL NOTES

VLADIMIR MAYAKOVSKY was born in April 1893 in Georgia, but moved with his family to Moscow in 1906 after the premature death of his father. In Moscow, he became involved in the activities of the Russian Social Democratic Labour Party (the Bolsheviks) and was imprisoned on three occasions for subversive political activities, although he avoided transportation because he was so young.

In 1911, he joined the Moscow Institute of Painting, Sculpture and Architecture where he became acquainted with members of the Russian Futurist movement – it was in the Futurist publication, *A Slap in the Face of Public Taste* (1912), that his first poems were published – although he was expelled from the Institute in 1914 because of his political activities. His reputation as a poet, both in Russia and abroad, was established in the period leading up to the Russian Revolution, with his first major poem, *A Cloud in Trousers*, appearing in 1915, the same year in which he fell in love with his publisher's wife, Lily Brik.

Rejected as a volunteer at the beginning of the First World War, Mayakovsky worked at the Petrograd Military Automobile School as a draughtsman, and was in Petrograd to witness the October Revolution. Moving back to Moscow, he worked for the Russian State Telegraph Agency (ROSTA), creating satirical Agitprop posters, and in 1919, he published his first full collection, *Collected Works 1909-1919*. Mayakovsky's popularity grew rapidly, both at home and abroad and, as one of the few Soviet writers allowed to travel freely, he visited Latvia, Britain, Germany, the United States, Mexico and Cuba, as well as travelling extensively in the Soviet Union itself. His influence on perceptions of poetry in early twentieth-century culture is hard to over-estimate.

During the 1920s, although regarded as a hero of the Soviet Union (his poetry was required reading for every Soviet schoolchild), Mayakovsky remained implacably opposed to bureaucracy and authoritarianism, a stance which resulted in official disapproval and restrictions on travel and other privileges.

On 14 April 1930, thoroughly disillusioned, Mayakovsky shot himself.

George Hyde was born in Scotland in 1941, son of an Army officer, and read English at Cambridge under the direction of F. R. Leavis, whose work on Tolstoy inspired him to learn Russian. Graduate work at Essex University with Donald Davie, who designed pioneering courses in comparative literature and literary translation, led to a teaching post at the University of East Anglia, where he helped Max Sebald set up the British Centre for Literary Translation. This was followed by a professorship at Kyoto Women's University, Japan, where he introduced comparative literature and culture courses. George Hyde also taught for four years at Polish universities in British Council funded posts during and after the communist period, and developed an interest in Polish theatre.

Publications include a study of the Russian heritage of Vladimir Nabokov, two books on D. H. Lawrence, and literary translation from Russian and Polish, as well as numerous essays in the field of Modernism. While in Japan, George Hyde published a number of essays on the neglected Norwich writer George Borrow, which will form the basis of a monograph.

In retirement, he is learning Greek and Japanese and has taken up the saxophone. He spends as much time as possible in his flat in Hania, Crete.

Larisa Molotova-Koroleva (pen-name Larisa Gureyeva) was born in May 1950 in Moscow, the granddaughter of Vyacheslav M. Molotov-Skryabin, Prime Minister of the Soviet Union from 1930-1939, then Foreign Secretary from 1939-1949 and 1953-1956. She began studying English at the age of eight, and graduated in English Philology and Literature at Moscow State University, before writing a postgraduate dissertation on Jane Austen and Iris Murdoch.

Her published work includes poetry (*The Stone Garden*, Moscow, 2001) and numerous translations of poetry, fiction, history and memoires. Her translation of *Love Story* (Moscow, 1990) went through three editions. At the time of publication, she is involved in a new publishing project, *Dolinskaya Storona*, which deals with the history of Vyatka (formerly Kirov), the Russian region close to the Urals. She is specialising in research on several dynasties of eighteenth- and nineteenth-century merchant families there.

Since 1979 she has been a member of the Moscow Writers' Committee, and she has been vice-chairperson of its poetry section since 1994. In February 1991, and again in April 1994, she visited the British Centre for Literary Translation (Norwich) as a recipient of bursaries.

Larisa Gureyeva's other interests include modern art (especially the Pre-Raphaelites, Art Nouveau, Jugendstil, and the Symbolists) and music. She is married to Sergei Korolev, a prominent heart surgeon.

JOHN WAKEMAN has published two poetry collections, *A Sea Family: New and Selected Poems* (Bradshaw Books, 2005) and *A Room for Doubt*, and his poems have appeared in many journals and anthologies. He co-founded, and for twelve years co-edited, the UK poetry magazine *The Rialto*. Moving to Ireland, he founded *The Shop – A Magazine of Poetry* which he now co-edits with his wife Hilary. He has edited major reference books on contemporary world literature and on world film directors, and has also published stories, essays and reviews and given radio talks on the BBC and RTE.

Lightning Source UK Ltd.
Milton Keynes UK
UKHW022333200820
368576UK00005B/33